A Gui ... ublishing

by Terry Freedman

ISBN 07457 0039 X

Kuma

A Guide to Desktop Publishing

Published by:

Kuma Computers Ltd
12 Horseshoe Park
Pangbourne
Berks
RG8 7JW

Tel 0734 844335
Fax 0734 844339

Printed in Great Britain by Loader Jackson, Arlesey.

Other Computing Titles From Kuma:

IBM PC & Compatible Micros

DTP Sourcebook - Fonts & Clip Art for the PC by J. L. Borman	07457 0030 6
PageMaker 4.0 for Windows by William B. Sanders	07457 0031 4
ZBasic Quick Reference Guide for PC & Mac by John Sumner	07457 0140 X
The Windows Guide Book by Gill Gerhardi, Vic Gerhardi & Andy Berry	07457 0041 1
A Practical Guide to Timeworks Publisher 2 on the PC by Terry Freedman	07457 0147 7
The DR DOS 6 Quick Start Guide by John Sumner	07457 0038 1
Illustrated DR DOS 6 - The First 20 Hours by John Sumner	07457 0044 6
The User's Guide to Money Manager PC by John Sumner	07457 0047 0
Breaking Into Windows 3.1 by Bill Stott & Mark Brearley	07457 0056 X
The Utter Novice Guide to GW Basic by Bill Aitken	07457 0045 4
The Utter Novice Guide to Q Basic by Bill Aitken	07457 0046 2
PagePlus Illustrated by Richard Hunt	07457 0062 4
DOS 5 Quick Start Guide by John Sumner	07457 0054 3

Commodore Amiga

Program Design Techniques for the Amiga by Paul Overaa	07457 0032 2
Intuition A Practical Programmers Guide by Mike Nelson	07457 0143 4
The Little Red Workbench 1.3 Book by Mark Smiddy	07457 0048 9
The Little Blue Workbench 2 Book by Mark Smiddy	07457 0055 1

Apple Macintosh

DTP Sourcebook - Fonts & Clip Art for the Mac by J. L. Borman	07457 0050 0
ZBasic Quick Reference Guide for PC & Mac by John Sumner	07457 0140 X
The Quark Book by Rod Lawton & Isaac Davis	07457 0052 7

Psion Organiser

Psion Organiser Deciphered by Gill Gerhardi, Vic Gerhardi & Andy Berry	07457 0139 6
Using & Programming the Psion Organiser by Mike Shaw	07457 0134 5
File Handling on the Psion Organiser by Mike Shaw	07457 0135 3
Machine Code Programming on the Psion Organiser 2nd Ed. by Bill Aitken	07457 0138 8
Psion Organiser Comms Handbook by Gill & Vic Gerhardi & Andy Berry	07457 0154 X

Psion Series 3

First Steps in Programming the Psion Series 3 by Mike Shaw	07457 0145 0
Serious Programming on the Psion Series 3 by Bill Aitken	07457 0035 7

Atari ST

Atari ST Explored 2nd Ed. by John Braga & Malcolm McMahon	07457 0141 8
Program Design Techniques for the Atari ST by Paul Overaa	07457 0029 2
Programming by Example - ST Basic by Dr. G. McMaster	07457 0142 6
A Practical Guide to Calamus Desktop Publishing by Terry Freedman	07457 0159 0
A Practical Guide to Timeworks on the Atari ST by Terry Freedman	07457 0158 2

Cambridge Z88

Z88 Magic by Gill Gerhardi, Vic Gerhardi & Andy Berry	07457 0137 X

Games

Sega Megadrive Secrets by Rusel deMaria	07457 0037 3
Sega Megadrive Secrets Volume 2 by Rusel deMaria	07457 0043 8
Corish's Computer Games Guide	07457 0150 7
Awesome Sega Megadrive Secrets	07457 0226 0

Sharp IQ 7000 & 8000

Using Basic on the Sharp IQ by John Sumner	07457 0034 9

A selection from our fast-expanding range - latest full details on request

Acknowledgements

The following products were used or mentioned in the production of this book:

Product	Trademark/copyright owned by
Ami	Lotus
Calamus	DMC
GFA Draft Plus 3	GFA Data Media UK
Hyperpaint	Atari Corporation
Imagecopy	Jeremy Hughes (The ST Club)
Kwikdraw	Paul Schimpf
Megapaint II	Tommy Software
Microsoft Works	Microsoft
New World PD Clip Art	John MacLaren
Pagemaker	Aldus
Pageplus	Serif
PC Paintbrush	Microsoft
Publisher	Microsoft
Quark	Quark Inc
That's Snap	Compo
That's Write	Compo
Timeworks Publisher 2	GST
Typeplus	Serif
Wincap	Brightbill-Roberts and Co. Ltd
Windows 3.1	Microsoft
Wordart	Microsoft

All trademarks are acknowledged.

About this book

The basic purpose of this book is to teach you about desktop publishing. The first part of the book explains what it is, and what its general principles are. Although this is, if you like, the "theory" part of the book, it does in fact contain a fair bit of practical advice.

The second part of the book consists of a number of projects which show you how to go about creating various types of document or special effects. I tried to base this part of the book on those DIY guides or car maintenance books which contain lots of stage-by-stage photographs. Even if your particular DTP program doesn't operate exactly in the way shown in the examples, there will be, hopefully, enough ideas and suggestions here to enable you to experiment with confidence.

What the book represents, in effect, is my attempt to write the book that I myself would have found useful - first, when buying a DTP program, and secondly when trying to learn more about how to use it.

The final part of the book is a glossary.

I hope you find the book useful.

I should like to express my thanks to the following people and organisations for their co-operation in the production of this book:

Jon Day and Tim Moore at Kuma Computers Ltd for their support - both practical and moral , and their patience;

The University of Cambridge Local Examinations Board for permission to reproduce the "Design Brief" from their Cambridge Information Technology module in Desktop Publishing;

John MacLaren, proprietor of the New World PD Library, for permission to use the picture on page 25.12;

Ray Amsterdam for proof-reading and answering a few esoteric technical questions;

Elaine, my wife, for proof-reading, attention to detail and useful suggestions, and for her forbearance and moral support.

How this book was produced

This book was written with That's Write on an Atari 1040 STE and Lotus Ami on a PC. The screen shots of Atari programs were obtained with That's Snap and Imagecopy. The screen shots of PC programs were obtained with Wincap and its associated utilities, and the Windows clipboard facility. The text was desktop published on a PC using Timeworks Publisher 2. It was printed on an OKI OL840 Postscript LED printer at 300 dpi.

Terry Freedman

October 1992

Contents

What is desktop publishing?

Lots of people talk about desktop publishing. Some of them **do** it. But what exactly **is** it?

Desktop Publishing (DTP) is a system for producing documents which incorporate text and graphics, and which enables you to make the text flow around the pictures. It is also a way of allowing you to change the appearance of the text - perhaps quite dramatically, as in the examples here:

Examples of text manipulation

In order to do desktop publishing, you need the following:

- A computer - more or less any personal computer will do, but the more powerful the better, as a rule
- A mouse
- A monitor (although sometimes you can get by with a television set)
- Suitable software (see below)

In addition, it's **extremely** useful to have a printer, although you can always send a floppy disk to an agency to print your work off.

A hard disk drive is often useful, and sometimes essential. For example, you can run Timeworks Publisher 2 on an Atari without a hard disk drive, but you cannot do so on a PC unless you **do** have a hard disk drive.

You may also want to consider a buying a scanner, for graphics work. But more of that later...

You will also need the following software:

- A desktop publishing program
- A word processing program (ideally)
- A painting or drawing program (ideally)

Greater detail about hardware and software requirements are given at the end of this chapter.

Why *desktop* publishing?

In theory, you can carry out desktop publishing on a desk, hence the name. In practice, by the time you've added a printer, space for drawing up rough designs and so on, you're likely to require a pretty **large** desk! Still, it's a far cry from the days when you needed a printing press, and therefore quite a large room, in order to obtain the same sort of results.

Speaking of printing presses, the onset of desktop publishing does **not** mean that commercial printers should start looking for other employment. For quality of output, especially when very high volume is needed, you can't beat a machine called an industrial typesetter. So for the sort of job where extremely high quality results are required, desktop publishing is a very quick and inexpensive way of getting proofs, ie rough drafts, which can be used as a basis for judging what the final result will look like.

In a similar way, you could design a letterhead (ie headed notepaper) on your desktop publisher, print it out on a laser printer, and give it to your local commercial printer to make a printing plate from. This would save you the cost of having the printing company carry out **all** of this process. Some commercial printers even use desktop publishers themselves in order to "fine tune" the document with the client before going through an expensive and time-consuming printing process. These companies may even be able to accept your disk containing the work to be printed, thus saving them time and you money.

What can you use a desktop publishing program for?

The short answer is: anything that you could use a typewriter, wordprocessor, or commercial printer for. To be a little more specific, though, the sorts of things that a desktop publishing program can be used for are:

- Personal stationery
- Business stationery
- Leaflets
- Posters
- Company reports
- Newsletters
- Books

Where does word processing fit in?

There are many word processors around today which can do many of the things that a desktop publishing package can do. In the "old" days, ie about two years ago (!), you bought a desktop publisher for the freedom it gave you to have different styles and sizes of typefaces, to flow the text around pictures, to make the text go in different directions instead of just horizontal, and a host of other things that could give your document a highly polished look.

Nowadays, however, word processors can do many of these things. In fact, there are some word processors which are very similar to desktop publishers in what they can do. These are known as "document processors", because they are designed in such a way that it's very easy to work on the whole document at once. For example, through the use of a device called "tagging", you can change the appearance of the whole document, or certain bits of it (such as headings) at the press of a key or two.

However, word processors and document processors are fundamentally different from desktop publishers. Word processors are basically text **handlers**. They're ideal for typing in text, swapping bits around, searching for certain bits of text (known as "strings") and replacing them with others, checking the document for spelling, words used and grammar... In other words, word processors are used for... processing words!

Desktop publishers, on the other hand, are intended for **formatting** text (and graphics), for example by having different styles and sizes of typefaces (known as "fonts" or "founts"), several columns and inclusion of pictures.

Perhaps the real distinguishing feature, though, is the control that desktop publishing packages give you over the **spacing** of the text. For example, many give you control over kerning (the process of altering the spacing between two specific letters in a word) and leading, pronounced "ledding", (the spacing between lines of text). Some allow you control over tracking as well, which is similar to kerning except that it applies globally, not just between two specific characters. No word processor gives you this type of control over layout.

Word processing and desktop publishing are by no means mutually exclusive. In fact, they complement each other: a very good way of working, for reasons explained later, is to type the text in a word processor first and desktop publish it afterwards. However, if your budget will only stretch to **one** decent program, you need to ask yourself which is more important: to be able to handle text very efficiently or to be able to change its appearance very creatively and easily.

If you want the former, you ought to be looking at word processors, perhaps with some desktop publishing-type features, such as being able to have pictures in your documents. If the latter, you should be looking at desktop publishing packages, perhaps with some word processing features, such as the ability to search for and replace text.

Appendix to Chapter 1: Basic Hardware and Software Requirements

If you're still at the stage of trying to decide what hardware or software to buy, or if you're thinking of expanding your set-up, then this section is for you. Otherwise just skip it and go on to Chapter 2.

Hardware

This section is as non-technical as possible. It is, if you like, almost a bluffer's guide to the hardware scene, in the sense that it gives you a brief run-down of the sort of things you should be looking for - and looking out for in advertisements.

For the most part, this section is concerned only with PCs, ie clones of IBM machines, although other types of computer are mentioned. There are various alternatives available, not the least important of which is the Apple Macintosh range. However, these others are outside the scope of this book.

If you haven't got a computer system at the moment, then you should decide what software you want to run and then buy the hardware that will run it. In other words, decide on your needs and then buy the equipment that will enable you to meet them.

Having said that, what are the minimum useful hardware requirements?

The computer

Computers can be classified in several ways, one of which is processing speed. This is expressed as, eg, 16 bit or 32 bit. The higher the number the more powerful the computer.

Another expression is the speed of the computer in Mhz. Thus 25 Mhz is faster, and therefore more desirable than 16 Mhz.

Another important variable is the processor itself, if you are looking at PCs. The 80286 processor, more commonly known as "286", is more or less defunct in the most technologically advanced countries. At the time of writing, the choice is between a 386 and a 486. As you might expect, the 486 is the more powerful of the two.

Finally, as far as the processor or heart of the computer is concerned, you'll be faced with the choice between, say, a 386SX and a 386DX. The DX is the more powerful of the two, but probably isn't worth spending the extra money on if it means having to make a sacrifice elsewhere - such as on the size of the hard disk.

Another choice you may be faced with is whether to have a cache. This is a facility whereby more of the computer's memory is allocated to the program in use, because it is is quicker for the computer to read from that than from the hard disk drive. The higher the size of the cache, the faster the computer will work (other things being equal), up to a size of 256K, after which the speed starts to decrease. The larger the cache the more expensive the computer will be.

The hard disk drive

With some desktop publishing programs you can get away without having a hard disk drive. However, it's much more efficient to have one even if you don't actually need one. DTP programs and the documents they produce tend to be quite large.

How large should the hard disk drive be? The absolute minimum is 40 megabytes (or 40 Mb). In fact, this is likely to be too small, especially if you are running Windows on a PC. Probably 80 Mb is the bare **comfortable** minimum: you'd be surprised at how quickly it will get used up! Graphics in particular take up a lot of disk space - sometimes a single picture can take up more space than is available on a floppy disk.

As with computer processors, there are various standards by which hard disk drives are judged. The minimum requirement is that it should have what is known as an "IDE" or a "SCSI" controller.

You should also check the disk access time - the time it takes for the computer to locate information on the disk. 17 ms (milliseconds) is about the lowest acceptable speed these days - 15 ms is even better.

Floppy disk drives

A popular size is the 1.4 Mb high density 3.5" disk, so ideally the computer should be able to handle this format. If it can, it will also be able to handle the 3.5" double density floppy disk, which can hold about 720,000 bytes (or 720K); ie about half of the high density disk.

The reason for preferring the 1.4 Mb disks is that they can store the most data - useful when it comes to backing up your work.

The monitor

One of the most important aspects of desktop publishing work is the speed of screen re-drawing. All this means is the speed at which images are drawn on the screen. Every time you go to another page, change the size of the page on the screen, or change the size of a picture, there is a delay while the images are re-drawn on the screen.

If you want to use a colour monitor, the ideal **basic** configuration for the monitor is 14" VGA. Better still is a Super VGA monitor, preferably with 1 Mb of Video RAM (VRAM) - this assists the computer to re-draw the screen quickly.

CAUTION! Make sure that a monitor which has a 1 Mb VRAM SLOT actually contains a 1 Mb VRAM CARD, as opposed to a 512 K card, which is half the size. It is not unknown for unscrupulous companies to supply you with something other than what you think you're buying.

If you can't afford a VGA or Super VGA monitor, an EGA monitor is a good runner-up if you can get hold of one - they are no longer being manufactured.

As it happens, you don't need a colour monitor for desktop publishing work. A high resolution monochrome monitor would be ideal if you don't require a colour monitor for your other programs.

If money is not a problem, you might go for a 17" monitor - or a 19" monitor, which will give you a much clearer display than a smaller monitor.

A problem which arises in the course of desktop publishing is that you usually have a choice between displaying the whole of an A4 page and actually being able to read it. You can select the size at which to view the page. For example, you could set the view size to **actual size**, which will display the text at the size it will print out at.

Alternatively, you could set the view size to **double size** or full page view . The double size view shows the page at twice the size it will be printed at - useful for detailed editing of graphics. The full page view shows the whole page at once, but the type is too small to read. In fact, some DTP programs represent the text as blocks. This is known as **greeking**.

Full page view

An advantage of a large screen is that it is possible to display a whole A4 page on the screen **and** be able to read it with ease.

You could even buy a monitor which will swivel on its side for displaying landscape (wide) documents.

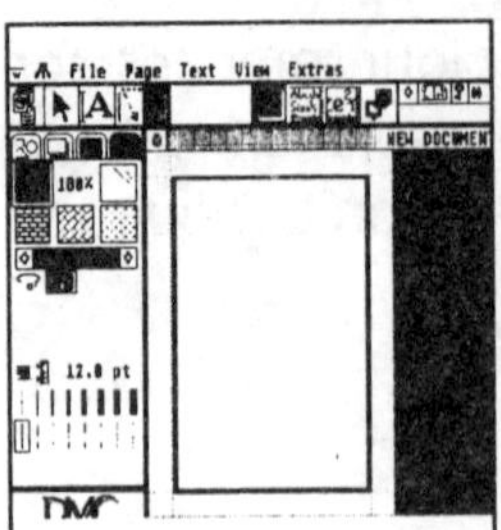

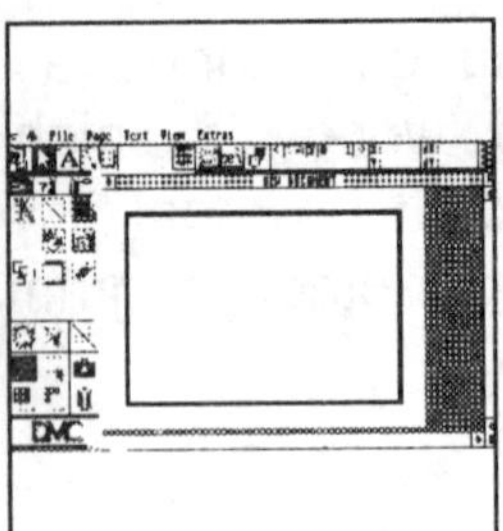

Far left:

Portrait orientation

Left:

Landscape orientation

Monitor specifications

Here is a summary of the main points to consider when purchasing a monitor for desktop publishing work. There are certain trade-offs which must be made, such as between a high resolution and a flicker-free image.

If you want...	Then pay attention to...
To see on the screen exactly what you'll get on the printout	the DTP software
To be able to enlarge the image on the screen for fine detail work	the DTP software
To be able to view one or two A4 pages on the screen at their actual size	size of screen
High screen resolution	pixel size and density; screen size; horizontal scan rate; phosphor persistence (the higher the better)
A flicker-free image	screen refresh rate; phosphor persistence (the lower the better); vertical scan rate; non-interlaced screen
Rapid redrawing of screen image	the DTP software; computer speed; video memory (VRAM); Graphics accelerator

Graphics standards*

MDA	Mono Display Adaptor	Text only
HGC	Hercules Graphics Card	Mono
CGA	Colour Graphics Array	Colour
EGA	Enhanced Graphics Array	Colour
VGA	Video Graphics Array	Colour
SVGA	Super Video Graphics Array	Colour

*A recent development is the XGA standard. See computer press for up-to-date details.

Technical terms used

In order to make this as practical a guide as possible, this is not a glossary but rather an indication of what to pay attention to when buying a monitor.

Horizontal scan rate

The higher the better. This is expressed in kHz. 1kHz = 1000 lines per second. SVGA should be around 35 kHz.

Interlaced/non-interlaced

Non-interlaced screens are quicker at redrawing the image and are less likely to cause flicker. See Vertical scan rate below.

Phosphor persistence

The screen is coated with phosphor, which emits light when scanned by an electron beam. If the phosphor light is too short-lived, screen flicker results. But if it persists too long, "ghosting" can result.

Pixel density

Pixels are the dots which make up the screen image. The smaller their size and the higher their density (ie number per unit area) the higher the resolution. Minimum requirement for serious desktop publishing work is 0.28 mm dot pitch.

Vertical scan rate

This is the rate at which the screen is redrawn. The higher it is, the less flicker there will be. In an SVGA monitor, the rate should be between about 45 kHz and 90 kHz.

Graphics accelerator

(Also known as video accelerator). This comes on a card which fits inside the computer. It contains instruction about how to draw lines. This means that it can get on with the task of redrawing the screen while the computer itself does something else. Consequently, both the screen graphics and the computer are speeded up.

The mouse

Some desktop publishing packages work without a mouse - but there are some operations for which, for all practical purposes, a mouse is essential. Usually, the correct mouse will be supplied with the computer. If it doesn't, it will be supplied as an optional extra. Either way, if you obtain the mouse at the same time as the computer you should not need to worry about whether it's compatible with the computer or not.

Tape streamer

It is essential to back up regularly the files you create. This can take a long time if you are backing up on to floppy disk drives - especially if you have a very large and very full hard disk drive. It is worth considering the purchase of a tape streamer. This is a device which backs the files onto what looks like a video tape. It is much faster than backing up onto floppies.

The keyboard

Keyboards come in various styles. The best one for use with a PC is a 102 key keyboard (in the UK). This features the standard QWERTY keyboard plus a number of extra keys. It also has a numeric keypad, which makes for very rapid input of figures.

The printer

Please see Chapter 10 for a discussion of printers and printing.

Summary of basic hardware requirements: an example

Here is an example of a hardware set-up which was put together from the "mix-and-match" service offered by many mail order companies.

- 486SX-25 with 4 Mb of RAM and 128K cache, and the following ports (sockets): 2 serial, 1 parallel, 1 games
- 3.5" High Density floppy disk drive

- 210 Mb hard disk drive
- 14" SVGA monitor with 1mb of VRAM
- 250 Mb tape streamer (also known as a tape drive)
- Mouse
- Enhanced "AT" style 102 key keyboard

This is not recommended as being ideal as such - after all, if the money was available you could go for a much faster and bigger system. However, it is extremely good for desktop publishing work, being quite fast and having a fair amount of memory (RAM) and hard disk space to play with.

Both the level of technology and the prices of hardware are changing all the time. For up to date product information the best thing to do is to consult the many excellent monthly magazines available.

Software

The DTP program itself

Before buying a DTP program, you need to work out what you wish to use it for. Do you intend producing books or other types of long, multiple page documents? Or do you intend to use it more for producing leaflets, posters and so on? Different types of document require different types of facilities. It is no good buying a very powerful - and expensive - package when you will only be using about 20 % of its potential. On the other hand, there's not much point in buying a bargain basement package which will not let you do everything you want to do.

Here is a list of the various types of document, followed by a list of the features a desktop publishing package ought to have in order to allow you to produce them. This is intended to be a guide-line rather than a definitive statement.

- Single sheet publications
- Stationery
- Newsletters
- Books, company reports, technical manuals

Single sheet publications

This category includes posters, which are typically A4 or A3 in size, and displayed on walls and notice-boards; flyers, which are smaller versions of posters - typically A5 in size; and leaflets, which are typically an A4 sheet folded in three and printed on both sides.

Stationery

Obviously, stationery could be regarded as part of the previous category. However, it's worth making a distinction between the two because of the slight differences in desktop publishing features required for the two types.

Stationery includes both personal stationery and business stationery. The latter also includes specialised stationery such as invoices and memos. Invoices and memos often include graphical features such as lines, and invoices usually incorporate several columns.

Newsletters

A newsletter may also be a single sheet, but is more complicated than the previous categories in terms of the number of desktop publishing features required. Multiple columns, text flowed around graphics and, usually, several pages are involved.

Books etc

These involve several pages (rather than just a single sheet), and therefore involve such features as headers and footers, page numbering, double vs single page layout and, possibly, multiple columns.

DTP features required for each type of document

	MK	LD	BD	G	TG	RT	ST	PN	DPL
Single Sheet	3	3	3	2	2	3	1	0	0
Stationery	1	3	2	2	1	2	1	0	0
Newsletter	2	3	3	3	3	2	3	1	1
Books	2	2	2	3	3	1	3	3	3

Keys to Table

0 Not necessary

1 Could be useful

2 Fairly useful

3 Essential

MK Manual Kerning - ie ability to adjust space between letters

LD Line Drawing

BD Box Drawing

G Guide-lines/Grid - ie visible, adjustable and "snappable-to"

TG Text flow around Graphics, esp. around irregular shapes

RT Rotated Text

ST Style Tagging-ie tagging information can be inserted into word-processed document

PN Page Numbering - ie pages can be numbered automatically, preferably in a variety of formats

DPL Double Page Layout - ie document can be set up for double-sided pages

Minimum requirements

As well as these suggested features, a desktop publishing package should have the following features as a bare minimum:

- Ability to show full size page view
- Automatic kerning
- Support for multiple columns
- Ability to import ASCII files
- Ability to import vector graphics, eg EPS files, and bitmap graphics, eg PCX or IMG
- Ability to save files in EPS format for output to a Postscript laser printer (See Chapter 10)
- Automatic timed back-up facility

"Optional extras"

There are many other types of features offered by some desktop publishing programs. Some have vast text handling facilities, such as the ability to have text size of 2000 points (for a single character to take up an A4 page it would need to have a size of about 700 points), or a powerful table of contents generator.

Others have their strengths on the graphics side, with extensive colour handling, import capabilities and drawing/retouching tools.

The operating environment - a note on Windows

One of the advantages of Windows is that you can use a facility known as object linking and embedding. Without going into a lot of technical details, what it means is that switching between applications is very easy, as is updating your work.

Suppose you draw a picture in PC Paintbrush and then import it into, say Microsoft Publisher, and at a later date you want to make alterations to the picture. If you have embedded it as an object in Microsoft Publisher, you can open PC Paintbrush by clicking on the picture in your document. If you have linked the picture, then you can alter the picture in PC Paintbrush and the picture in your Microsoft Publisher document will be updated automatically.

Summary

Before purchasing desktop publishing software...

- Sit down and think what you will using it for mainly
- Write down the sorts of features you require, using this chapter as a guide-line
- Decide upon your maximum expenditure;
- Find the right program! (Some suppliers can provide demonstration versions of their programs so that you can "try before you buy" as it were).

If you haven't any computer hardware yet, shop around for the hardware that will run your chosen software package.

Other useful software

You ought to have certain other software as well in order to undertake serious desktop publishing. The other programs you should consider are:

- A word processing program
- A painting or drawing program

plus, perhaps,

- A graphics format converter
- A screen capture utility

Suggested minimum features of these programs

Here are some suggestions as to what to look for in each of these programs, if you are considering buying them. Note that the features listed are those which are considered important from a desktop publishing standpoint. If you want a particular application in its own right, there are many other features you will want to look for, and which are not covered here.

Word processor (or text editor)

This should have...

- The facility for saving in ASCII format, preferably with several options (eg carriage feed at the end of each paragraph, or the end of each line)
- A good spell-checker (ie one which is based on a dictionary that has a good store of words and which you can add to)

- A search and replace facility
- Automatic timed back-up, preferably
- A macro facility (for assigning commands and text to keyboard "hot" keys)

A painting or drawing program

This should have...

- The ability to save and load files in a variety of popular formats, such as TIFF, PCX, IMG for bitmap packages, and EPS,GEM,CGM for vector graphics programs
- The facility for varying line widths and fill patterns
- The facility for incorporating text in the drawing, so that when you resize the drawing the text is resized as well (preferably)

A graphics format converter

This is a utility which can load a picture in one format and save it in another format. For example, the program used to capture the Windows screens featured in this book had an accompanying utility to convert the pictures to PCX format. This enabled them to be loaded into a painting program to have the colours changed to black and white for the sake of greater clarity.

Sometimes you can use a painting program to do the conversion. For example, the screen shots of Timeworks Publisher and Calamus in this book were taken with a utility which saved them in Degas (PI3) format. They were then loaded into a painting program called Hyperpaint and saved in IMG format. They were then imported into the Timeworks Publisher document on a

PC.(The pictures had to be converted from PI3 format to IMG format because the PC version of Timeworks Publisher 2 does not accept PI3 format graphics).

A screen capture utility

This is a program that takes snapshots of the computer screen for incorporation into technical manuals or "how to..." books.

Note that there are several varieties available in the PC world, for taking screen shots from within DOS-based programs, Windows-based programs and GEM-based programs.

The basic features a screen capture program must have are...

- The ability to save screens in a popular format, or a format which can be easily converted into a popular format
- The ability to capture drop- or pull-down menus when in a GEM or Windows environment
- The ability to save screens with the minimum of fuss - and certainly without having to exit from the program you're in
- The facility for saving screens with an incremental name, eg SCRNDMP1, SCRNDMP2 and so on

Other software

There is bound to be other software which you will find useful as you continue to do desktop publishing. For example, you may come across a handy utility that will format a blank disk for you in the background while you are working on something.

However, the software mentioned here will provide a sound basis for getting started, and for a quite a long time after that in all likelihood.

What does desktop publishing involve?

There are a number of stages involved in the desktop publishing process. That isn't to say that everyone carries them out to the letter every time they want to do some desktop publishing: quite often, a person will just get straight on to the computer and work on a trial and error basis.

That's definitely a more spontaneous approach, but it can also lead to a lot of time being wasted. It's a matter of personal preference whether you adopt the fairly structured approach explained below, or a more spontaneous one. However, it's probably worth saying that it's better to learn the rules before attempting to break them!

Here, then, is the formal or structured version of the desktop publishing process.

1. Consider what needs to be done, for whom, why, and by when. This is called the "Design Brief", and is elaborated on below.

2. Design the layout. ie, work out how the document should look, where the pictures (if any) should go, and so on. It's not a bad idea to use paper and a pencil at this stage.

3. Set up the pages with margins, text frames and any other frames. See Chapter 3 for an explanation of what frames are..

4. Put the text in.

5. Put the pictures in.

6. Change the text styles/fonts and/or reformat the document.

7. Save the document and/or layout and/or pages.

8. Print the document.

The text can be typed in directly or "imported", ie brought in, from a word processed file.

The picture will have to be created beforehand, and then "imported", ie brought into the document.

This is, as you can see, a fairly logical approach. Of course, it doesn't usually work out so neatly in practice.

Take, for example, stage 2, in which you decide what the layout of the document is going to be. You can take the planning of this only so far: there comes a point where you simply have to get on with desktop publishing the document and see what it looks like, and make adjustments if necessary. (Adjustments are **always** necessary!).

Bear in mind also that printing the document is usually a part of the process, not just the end of it. At various stages - after stage 2, for instance - you'll probably want to obtain a rough printout (known as a "draft") in order to check the appearance of the document.

At a later stage you may want to obtain another draft printout, this time to check whether the graphics look OK, or to proof-read the text again. The first stage, referred to as the "Design Brief", is quite a large thing in itself, as explained now...

The Design Brief - summary

Before explaining what this consists of, let's just look at the meaning of the name itself.

Imagine someone above you in your place of work gives you an assignment to carry out. It may be, for example, "Find out the names of all our customers who owe more than £300". That is a "brief".

When applied to desktop publishing, the term "brief" refers to the instructions governing the production of a document.

The brief may be, for example, "Produce a report on last month's sales figures for distribution to everyone in the Section."

You now have to to work out how to produce the document, what it will look like, how best to have it reproduced (eg photocopying or offset litho?), all by a deadline.

These decisions/questions are often collectively referred to as the "Design Brief". Overleaf is a summary of these questions, followed by a detailed explanation.

- Who is the target readership?
- What is the publication intended to achieve?
- What (underlying?) message will be given by the publication?
- What text files will be required?
- What illustrations will be required?
- What is the overall format?
- What typefaces will be used, and why?
- What are the printing specifications?
- How will the publication be reproduced?
- What are the publishing deadlines?

Now, not all of these will be relevant for every publication, so don't feel you must answer all of these questions every time you want to use your desktop publishing package! Also, it's worth bearing in mind that most of the time you will be giving **yourself** the design brief, or the greater part of it.

It is not unusual for the person asking you to do the desktop publishing work to be astonishingly vague about their requirements. Instructions such as "Can you desktop publish this report by Friday please? Make it look really nice" are not unheard of! When you receive instructions like this, use the Design Brief to help you get down to the "nitty gritty", and to help you translate into practice descriptions like "nice".

If **you** are the one who wants the work done, you can still use the Design Brief for the same purpose. Now here is a more in-depth look at what the Design Brief is all about.

The Design Brief explained

Who is the target readership?

Which age groups, which sex; shareholders? customers? potential clients? It isn't only things like the kind of language used that could differ between different target audiences. Other features, such as the font(s) used, size of print, graphics must also be considered. In order to make life easier when you come to deal with other questions in the Design Brief, it's a good idea to be as precise as you can at this stage.

For example, the publication may be intended for parents of children at a secondary school, in order to inform them about the activities and achievements of the school during the past year. Presumably, the same information would be conveyed in a completely different format to the Governors of the school, or a team of Inspectors.

What is the publication intended to achieve?

To shock? To inform? What?

What message will be given by the publication?

The same information may be conveyed in different formats depending on the purpose of the publication. Taking the example of a summary of a school's activities, a publication for parents may be intended to inform them, on one level. On another level, the massage may be:

"Tell all your friends about about wonderful school so that lots of people apply to send their children here."

The message to be conveyed to a team of Inspectors would probably be rather different - something along the lines of:

“See what a professional and efficient organisation we have here, one which enables the pupils to reach their full potential in all aspects of their school lives.”

The message to be conveyed will influence choice of fonts, graphics and layout. A publication with lots of boxes, graphics, fonts and so on - in other words a publication which appears very “busy” - will give a rather different impression to one which is plain and simple.

One isn’t better or worse than the other in itself, but it’s important to know in advance what sort of (hidden?) message you want to get across - and, of course, the techniques you might use to achieve your goals.

"Hidden" messages are conveyed by the layout, the choice of fonts, the general layout - every aspect of the document’s appearance, in fact.

As an example of this, look at the illustrations opposite. The same text and the same border were used in all four cases, but the typefaces differ. How does that fact change the impression created in each case?

The quick brown

The quick brown

The quick brown fox jumped

The quick brown fox

Changing the font changes the underlying impression. Starting at the top left the fonts used are Times Roman, a classic-looking typeface; Chicago, which is modernistic; Barnum, with shades of the Wild West; and Universal Medium, a quietly modern typeface.

What text files will be required?

It's important to make a list of what text files will be needed and make sure they're to hand. This applies even if you're writing the publication as well as desktop publishing it. If you're not writing or word processing the files yourself, you may need to make sure that the person who is knows how to save the text files in the correct format - usually ASCII. (See Chapter 4).

Text files may be being prepared by different people. Have they been given a deadline by which to have the files ready? (Work backwards from your own deadline, and allow a good margin of error).

Where are the text files stored? What are they called? It will be a great help to you if the names of the text files bear some relation to the publication itself. For example,

"INSPRPTU.TXT", to denote the report for the Inspectors on university admissions, is rather more useful than "FRED1.TXT" ! Similarly, if all relevant files are saved on the same disk, or in the same directory or folder on the hard disk, your job will be much easier than if they're scattered all over the place. **(But make sure you have backups stored elsewhere!)**

Up to now, it has been assumed implicitly - for the most part anyway - that there's team work involved. However, even if you are working on your own these considerations still apply. For a long-ish piece of text, ie more than an A4 page's worth, it's much more efficient to word process the document first, and **then** desktop publish it, rather than typing directly into the desktop publisher. Why? Because not only is it faster (usually) - you can take advantage of the (usually) superior text-handling facilities of your word processor.

A bit of careful planning can make the whole desktop publishing process much smoother. For example, you may find it quicker to omit the title of the publication from your word processed file, so that you can type it straight into a special "frame" or box. (Explained in Chapter 3).

What illustrations will be required?

Similar considerations apply to image files as to text files, plus a few additional ones:

- Do the graphics depend on the text or other files?

For instance, are the graphs generated directly from statistical data?

- What form will the images take?

For example, will they be on disk or on paper? If the latter, are they going to be pasted in or scanned in?

- Are the graphics being prepared by a third party?

If so, do **they** know what the deadlines are? Graphics are covered in more detail in Chapter 5.

What is the overall format?

This aspect is dealt with more specifically in Chapter 3, in the sections on style sheets and master pages. It refers to considerations like the size of the paper to be used, and whether the pages are going to be all the same, or different between left and right pages.

Taking the question of page size first, there are several factors that may have to be considered.

For example, if you are producing an A5-size leaflet, you might consider desktop publishing it on an A4-size page layout with landscape orientation, ie with the longer edges along the top and bottom and the shorter edges at the sides. Sometimes, there are certain conventions to consider. For example, dissertations/reports are usually produced on A4 paper, whereas computer manuals are usually produced on the US equivalent of A5 paper. Sometimes, you may want to work on an A4 page layout, and then reduce or enlarge the finished document in a photocopier.

What typefaces will be used, and why?

This relates to the points made earlier about message conveyed by the publication. Different typefaces convey different messages. This is explained in more detail in Chapter 7, but for now have a look at the illustrations below and ask yourself how the change in typefaces changes the message conveyed by the publication.

A History of
Essex
Part 3: The
Middle Ages
by
Agnes
Grunthorpe

A History of Essex
Part 3:
The Middle Ages
by
Agnes Grunthorpe

A History of
Essex
Part 3:
The Middle
Ages
by
Agnes
Grunthorpe

Going in a clockwise direction from top left, the fonts used are Universal Medium, Times 100 and Old German.

What are the printing specifications?

- Colour or black and white?
- What type of paper?
- Final printout or draft printout?

How will the publication be reproduced?

This is very important, because it can affect the way you make the document look. Suppose, for example, the document is to be reproduced by offset litho. A problem that can occur with this method is that if there is too much black on the page, the offset litho machine can over-ink it, with the result that even areas that were supposed to be clear come out black, and/or sharp black lines become fudged.

However the publication is going to be reproduced, see the person who'll be doing it as early as possible to ascertain what difficulties, if any, could arise. Another reason for seeing the reprographics person is to find out how long they will need to complete the work. This, of course, will have an effect on the deadlines you set for other people's work.

What are the publishing deadlines?

Don't forget - whatever deadlines you've been given will have an effect on the deadlines **you** set for other people. You may also need to take into account the time required for distribution of the publication - For example, a couple of days for postal delivery.

Finally, you may need to cost it out (and have the cost approved in advance). This is another reason for seeking an early appointment with the person in charge of the reprographics end. It may be that photocopying costs three times as much as offset litho reproduction, but that there is a minimum number of copies required to make offset litho economically viable. At a certain point, it may be worthwhile to have a few more reproduced in order to enjoy the cost advantages.

Let's take a simple example:

In **Company A plc** you are charged 3 pence per photocopy and 1 penny per offset lithographed page. However, you can only have something reproduced by offset litho if you want more than 30 copies. You need 30 copies of a 10 page document. If you have it photocopied, the cost will be: 30 x 10 x £0.03 = £9.00.

However, if you have 50 copies by offset litho, it will cost you: 50 x 10 x £0.01 = £5.00, or virtually half price. **And** you have a few spares!

Other people

People who don't know much about desktop publishing have a tendency to think it's easy. Impossibly vague instructions and laughable deadlines are frequently the order of the day. Unfortunately, these very people are usually above us in rank and so cannot easily be told to jump in the lake!

You can help them to be more specific in stating their requirements by having examples of work to show them. Then you can say things like "Do you want it to look like **this**, or like **this**?". Every time you complete a desktop publishing assignment, keep a copy for yourself (if you can). In that way you'll build up a portfolio of examples which you can use in the way suggested.

So much, then, for the planning side of desktop publishing. What about the way you actually **use** a desktop publishing package? That's the subject of the following chapter.

How DTP Packages Work: Basic Principles

There are two basic types of desktop publishing program: those which make use of a device called a frame, and those which do not make use of frames.

Frame-based programs

A frame is a box into which you place text or a graphic. Usually, in order to place text or graphics on the page you must draw a frame first, although sometimes the program will do this for you automatically.

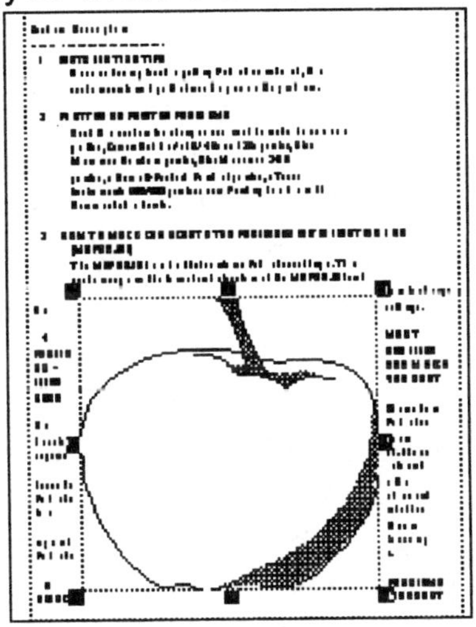

A frame-based program. The picture and the text are in different frames. Note the black squares around the picture, indicating that the frame has been selected and can now be moved around... (See Ch.6)

Once the text or graphic is in a frame you can move the frame - and therefore its contents - about, either within a single page or between pages in a document. Some packages let you move the frames about between documents too.

Some desktop publishing packages have different types of frame for different types of contents. That is, there is a special type of frame for vector graphics, another type for text, and so on. Other packages

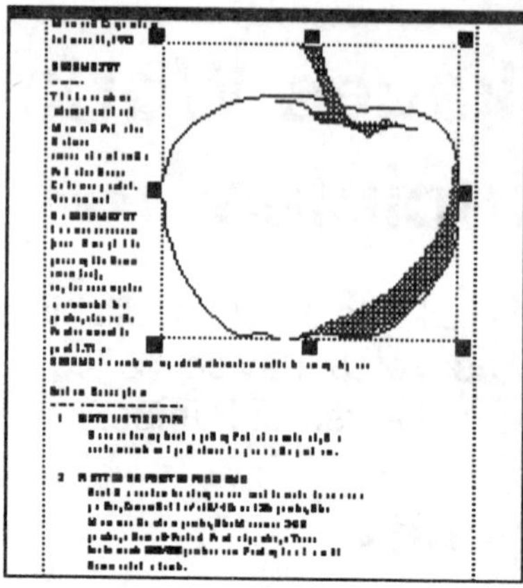

...Now the picture has been moved simply by moving the frame containing it.

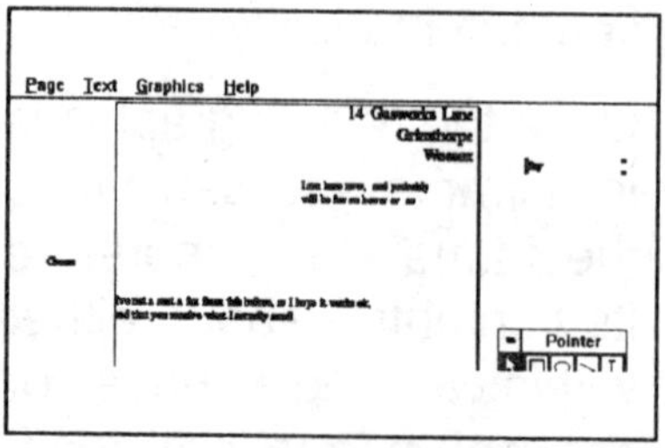

Here there are no frames as such - although they are created automatically when you wish to move something.

just have one all-purpose frame type. The former gives you a wider range of control over what you can do, but the latter is easier to use because there's less to think about.

Non-frame programs

An increasing trend these days is for desktop publishing packages to not use frames as such, but to allow you to type directly onto the page. Several Windows programs have this feature.

In such programs, you can place the text or graphic anywhere you like on the page straight away. If you decide to move it later on, you simply point to the block of text or the graphic with the mouse, press and hold the left mouse button, and move it to where you want it. When you carry out this operation, a frame will automatically form around the text or the graphic.

Which type of package is better? Each system has its advocates and detractors. The two most widely used systems in industry - Pagemaker and Quark - use a non-frame system and a frame system respectively. Neither package has suffered falling sales because of the system used. This would seem to suggest that neither system is better, in any objective sense, than the other.

The pasteboard analogy

Both types of system often make use of the pasteboard analogy. In traditional page make-up and typesetting, text and illustrations are laid out on a board with the blank page in the middle. Text and graphics are moved from the pasteboard area - the area around the blank page - to the page itself. In other words, text and graphics can be stored on the pasteboard until needed.

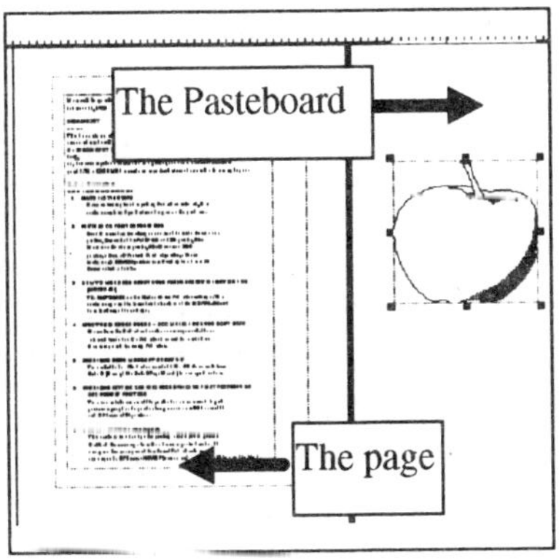

The electronic pasteboard: the page is surrounded by a storage area where you keep text and pictures until they are needed.

In the same way, the page make-up artist using a desktop publishing program can have all the text and graphics required on hand, and is able to place them and move them between the electronic equivalent of the pasteboard as needed.

All desktop publishing packages work according to certain common principles. These common elements are:

- Style sheets
- Master pages
- Importing
- Exporting

Style sheets

A style sheet is a set of instructions which tells the desktop publishing package how to lay out your documents. For example, you may want all your documents to have a left hand margin of 2cm and a 4-column layout. (See Chapter 8 for examples of different layouts). To save yourself the bother of having to configure this layout every time you start a new document, you need do it only once, as a style sheet. Then, every time you start a new document, you instruct the program to use that style sheet as the basis for the document's layout.

You may wish to have several style sheets for different types of document, eg reports, cover sheets, posters, tickets and so on.

As well as saving you time and trouble, style sheets also help to ensure that the appearance of your documents is fairly consistent. This is quite important in the business world, where companies develop their own "house style".

Some desktop publishing packages do not use style sheets as such, but have a facility for saving layouts. It amounts to the same thing: when starting a new document, instead of loading a style sheet, you load a layout instead.

Style sheets usually contain details of the master page(s) too...

Master pages

Just as style sheets govern the overall appearance of a document or several documents, so master pages govern the layout of pages **within** a document.

For example, if you want the pages to be numbered, with the page number appearing in the same place on each page, you will probably need to set this up on the master page(s). Because all subsequent pages are copies of the master page(s), the page number will come out in the same position on every page.

You can have just one master page for a document, in which case all the pages will look the same, or TWO master pages - one for left (even-numbered) pages and one for right (odd-numbered) pages.

If you have left and right pages, you no longer have "left" and "right" margins but "inner" (nearest the spine) and "outer" (nearest the edge) margins.

Master pages contain details of the headers and footers. A header is a piece of text which appears at the **top** of each page, while a footer is a piece of text appearing at the **bottom** of each page.

In some desktop publishing packages the term "master page" is not actually used. In these cases, look for a facility for saving individual pages within a document, or for saving templates. The basic idea is exactly the same, but instead of loading a previously-saved layout when starting a new document, you load a previously-saved page instead.

Importing

The concept of importing is central to desktop publishing. Desktop publishing itself is really a kind of document formatting factory. You "feed" it raw materials in the form of text and graphics, and the finished product comes out at the other end.

This act of bringing in text and/or graphics which were created within some other program is known as "importing".

Exporting

This is the opposite of importing. It is where work done in the desktop publishing program is saved in a form which can be read by another program, or inserted into another document.

Style Sheets and Master Pages

Style sheets contain details of:

- page format, eg A4, A3

- paragraph styles, eg Helvetica 12 point bold, indented

- master pages, ie headers, footers, and anything else which is meant to appear on every page.

For example...

You may have a **style sheet** called REPORT for your company reports. This contains details of the page format etc. For instance, every Report will be on A4 paper in portrait orientation and contain 6 paragraph styles and their associated fonts.

However, each Report will be different from the others because it will have a different **master page**.

For instance, the header on one will say September 1992, while in another Report it will be January 1993.

Despite these relatively superficial differences due to the differences in the master pages employed, the Reports all have a similar appearance because the same style sheet has been used throughout.

Suppose you typed some text directly into the desktop publishing program, and then decided to edit it in a word processor.

You would export it in what is known as "ASCII format" (See chapter 4), and then start up your word processor program and **import** the text into it.

Alternatively, you may want to save the text in a form which retains its formatting (eg **bold**, *italics* etc) so as to be usable in another desktop publishing document with the minimum of fuss. This time, you will want to export it in a different format from ASCII.

Note that whereas all desktop publishing packages have importing facilities, not all have exporting facilities. And the ones that do often don't have a very sophisticated or extensive set of exporting options. The reason for this is quite straightforward: since you've almost certainly already created the text or graphics in another program, you're less likely to want or need to **export** it from a desktop publishing program than to **import** it into a desktop publishing program.

Default settings

Many desktop publishing packages have a facility for setting defaults, ie a set of options that will be put into effect automatically whenever you start a new document.

In Timeworks Publisher 2 for example, you can set the program up to load a particular style sheet automatically when you start the program, to look in a particular place when importing text files, to save documents in a particular place and to save automatically at intervals of your choosing, plus several other options.

The desktop publishing environment

As indicated earlier working with an electronic desktop publishing system is analogous to working with a traditional one. You start with a blank page, and you have various bits of text and pictures that have to be put on the page and moved around until all concerned are satisfied. The obvious difference between the two systems is that one is "for real", in the sense that you can see and touch all the tools and page contents you will need, whereas in the other system everything is represented on a screen.

WIMPs

All desktop publishing programs use some form of WIMP environment. WIMP stands for:

Windows

Icons

Menus

Pointers

Windows

Not necessarily the Microsoft environment. In this context "windows" means any GUI - Graphic User Interface. On the page opposite are two examples of GUIs.

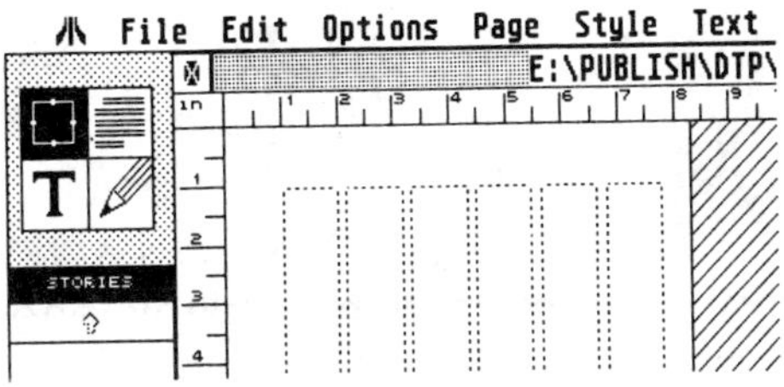

The GUI environment of Timeworks Publisher

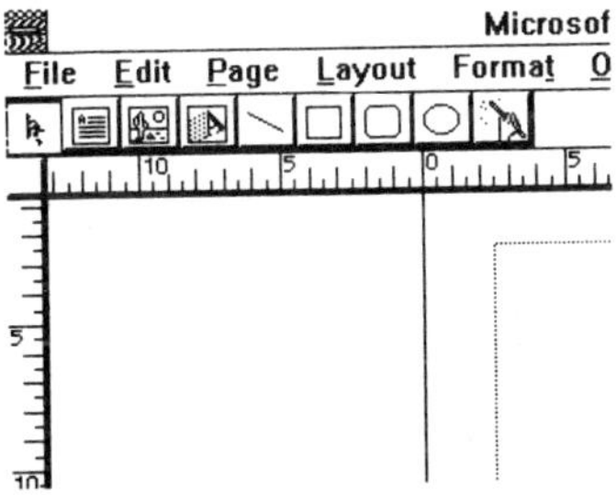

The GUI environment of Microsoft Publisher

Icons

Tools are represented on the screen is through the use of little pictures, or "icons". These are sometimes very obvious in their meaning, as when a camera is used to represent a copying facility. At other times, they are somewhat obscure. It's advisable to always look up the meaning of incomprehensible icons, just in case you click on one which deletes all your work!

Examples of the kind of icons used in desktop publishing programs

Menus

Another distinguishing feature of a windows or GUI environment is the use of menus from which you can select options.

An example of a menu. The grey items are not available to the user at the moment.

Menus may be either "drop down" or "pull down". If they are "drop down", they will appear as soon as the mouse pointer touches their names at the top of the screen. If they are "pull down", you have to point with the mouse to the menu's name, and then click the left mouse button.

Sometimes there are sub-menus, and even sub-sub-menus. The more sophisticated programs enable you to use keyboard shortcuts for each menu item.

Pointers

The mouse, too, does quite a bit in this system: there are usually at least five types of mouse pointer available in a DTP program:

- The normal arrowhead, used to select icons and menu items
- A cross, used to draw frames
- A flat hand, used to move frames
- A pointing finger, used to resize frames
- An I-beam, which acts as a text cursor

In addition, there may be other sorts of pointers. In Pagemaker, for example, when you import text the mouse pointer takes the shape of a page of text, which you have to place in the area where you want it to appear on the page.

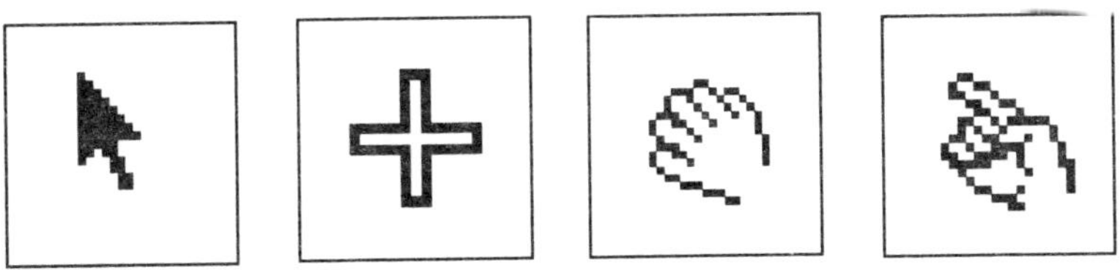

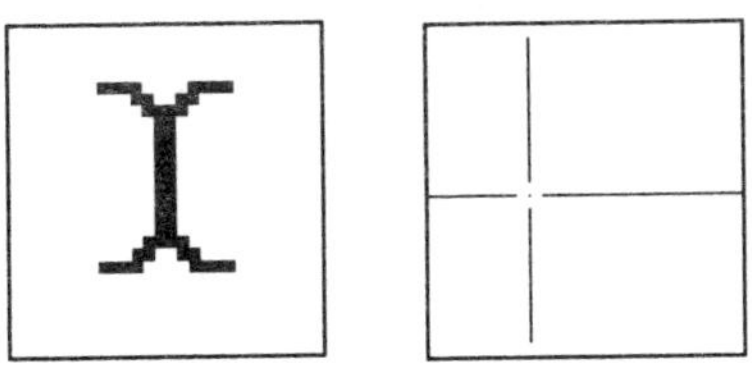

Examples of the various types of mouse pointer. Going from left to right we have - top row: arrowhead, cross, flat hand, pointing finger; bottom row: I-beam, cross-hairs.

Another kind of mouse pointer is the cross-hairs used by Calamus (optionally) instead of the (smaller) cross, since it lends itself to greater accuracy in the drawing and positioning of frames.

Once you've been using a DTP program for a while, the various ways of using the mouse, and the use of icons, will become second nature to you!

These, then, are the standard features found in most desktop publishing packages.

In the following two chapters, we look at how to handle text and pictures respectively.

Preparing Text for Desktop Publishing

In the first chapter of the book it was suggested that you buy a word processor even if your main interest is in desktop publishing. Why? It comes back to the statement made earlier that word processors are best at **handling** text while DTP programs are best at **formatting** it. This isn't always the case, but as a general rule it is true. Therefore it makes sense to do the bulk of the typing in a word processor, where you can spell-check the document, move paragraphs around, search for and replace text and so on, in a program that was actually designed to all that.

The other side of this coin is that you should reserve typing straight into the desktop publisher for small corrections/amendments to the text, or for inserting the odd line such as a heading, and not for great chunks of text.

So the way you work is to type the text, or most of it, in a word processor. Then, once you've made sure it reads the way you want it to, start up the desktop publisher and load the text into it. This is known as "importing" the text.

Saving files in the correct format

When you use a word processor, it puts invisible codes into the document. These codes contain information about things like page length, margin settings and text style (eg **bold**, *italics*, underlining etc).

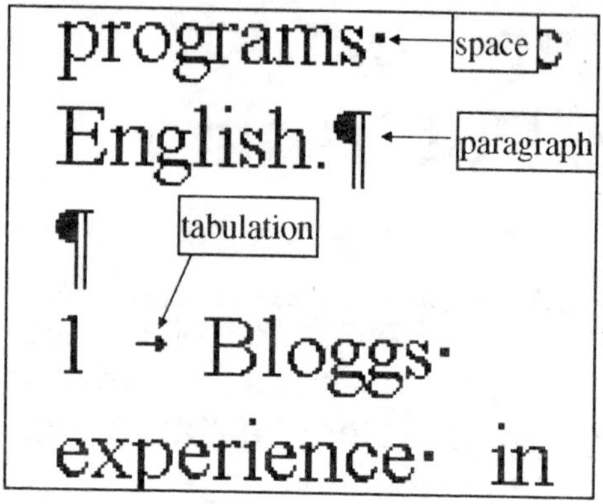

Some of the (usually invisible) codes that word processors place in documents. In order of appearance: space mark, end of paragraph (carriage return) mark and tabulation mark.

Invisible codes are all very well, until you attempt to read the document in another word processor, or a desktop publisher. In many cases you'll get a lot of rubbish in the document - if you're able to load it at all. In order to avoid these situations, you must save the word processed document without any of these invisible codes.

Before worrying about this, just check whether your desktop publisher will, in fact, import files directly from your word processor.

For example, Aldus Pagemaker will accept files processed in Microsoft Word, and Timeworks Publisher 2 will accept files processed in First Word Plus. (Each of these desktop publishing programs accepts files produced in other word processors too). If it does, you can skip this section and go straight on to the one on **Tagging paragraphs** (page 4.4).

If you save a file without these invisible codes then any other word processor or desktop publishing package should have no trouble in reading the file. (However, if different computers are used, make sure that the disk itself can be read by **both** computers).

A document saved in this way is known as an ASCII (pronounced "Asskey") file.

"ASCII" stands for American Standard Code for Information Interchange. Without going into a lot of technical detail, ASCII files consist of the text only, with none of the invisible codes referred to earlier. That means you lose attributes like bold type and underlining, but it also means that the document can be read by any word processor or desktop publisher.

If your word processor does not appear to have a command like "Save in ASCII", look out for one of the following:

- Save as text only
- Save without formatting
- Save unformatted
- Print to disk
- Give

If you cannot find any such command, you could always try looking in the manual!

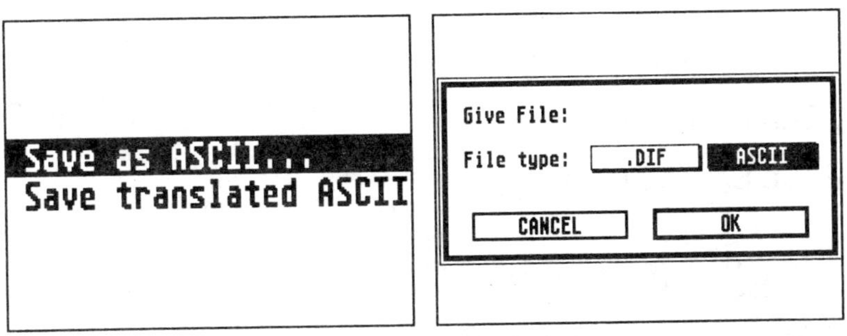

Examples of different terminology used for saving files in ASCII format.

Tabs, spaces and lines

If your desktop publisher accepts files straight from your word processor, you can skip this section. If, however, you must save the text in ASCII format, this section is quite important.

If anything is guaranteed to waste time, it's putting lots of spaces and tabs into the word processed document, because more often than not they have to be deleted in the desktop publisher and then put back in again from within the program. If you think about it, time has been wasted twice over - once while the text is being word processed, and again when the spaces etc are being taken out.

If someone else is doing the word processing, make sure that he or she is told not to put tabs, extra spaces and extra lines in, but to mark such attributes on a printed copy instead.

As an example, if the final text is to look like this:

1 The First Point

2 The Second Point

etc, then type it like this:

1The First Point

2The Second Point

Tagging paragraphs

One of the worst aspects of desktop publishing is the time it can take to change the appearance of certain parts of the text, as in making sub-headings larger than the main text. There are ways of speeding up these things within the desktop publisher itself but you may be able to "tell" the desktop publishing program what to do in the document itself.

Some desktop publishing packages allow you to assign styles to the text while it's being word processed. This is known as "tagging". Timeworks, for instance, enables you to tag the text like this:

<headline>The Old Values

There are three periods involved, which are:

<bullet>The Early Period

<bullet>The Middle Period

<bullet>The Late Period

<subhead>The Early Years

(Where there is no tag, normal or body text is assumed).

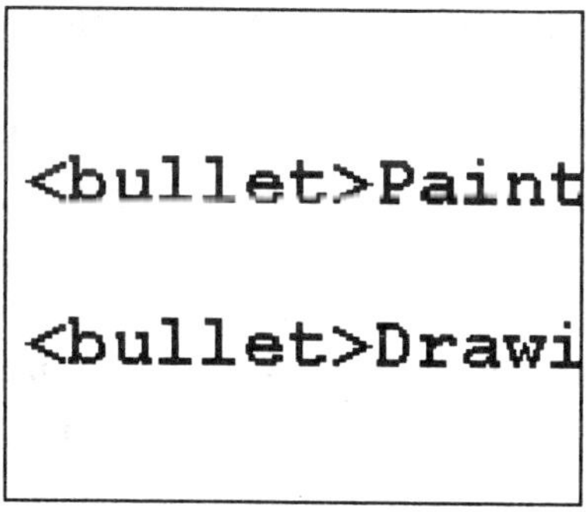

Examples of tagging the text.

When you import the text into Timeworks, the tags, ie "<subhead>" etc, do not appear on the screen. Instead, it becomes an invisible code which tells Timeworks that the text is a subheading or whatever, and so it's automatically formatted in the desired style. In fact, even if you haven't yet decided what attributes the paragraph style will have, it doesn't matter: as soon as you decide, and make the necessary changes, every block of text tagged with that style will change.

This technique of tagging the text in advance, as it were, can save much time and trouble. It is certainly much quicker to do this than to go through the document " by hand" reformatting every block of text that's meant to be a subheading.

What if your desktop publisher doesn't have a tagging facility? You can still make life easier for yourself by introducing your own form of tagging. For example, if you place an "<S>" in front of every piece of text that is going to be a subheading, you can locate each one very quickly in the desktop publisher by using the SEARCH option (sometimes called "FIND"). Simply "tell" the desktop publisher to find every instance of <S> in the document: usually, the way it works is that the first one is found and then you tell the program to repeat the search (perhaps using a special key combination such as Alt + R).

You may be able to use a macro to format the text into subheadings etc. Basically, a macro is a keystroke or keystroke combination which carries out certain instructions. In this example, suppose you wanted every subheading to be in a font called Universal medium, size 16 points (known as 16pt) and centred. All this information could be summarised as, say, Control + S. In that case, all you'd have to do is locate the text to be changed, highlight it, and press Control + S. This can save a great deal of time and repetition - especially in a very long document.

ctrl+shift+B	**bullet**
ctrl+shift+T	**table**
ctrl+shift+2	**bullet2**

Examples of macros: commands or text assigned to keyboard "hot keys".

Dingbats

Dingbats, or bullets, are symbols used to separate items in a list, draw your attention to an item of text or simply to "jazz up" the page. For example, a pointing finger might be used to indicate that the text is continued overleaf, or a picture of a telephone could be used instead of "Tel".

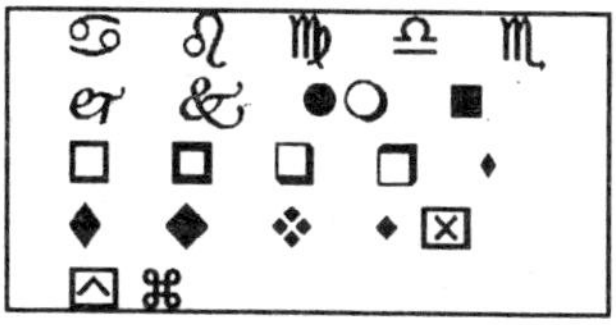

All of these symbols can be accessed from the keyboard if you have the requisite font

The usual technique for using dingbats is that you load the dingbat font (ie set of characters) into the desktop publisher program and click on the character you want. However, closer inspection will reveal that the symbol is, in fact, an ordinary keyboard character which is interpreted in a particular way by the dingbat font. Knowing this, you can save yourself a bit of time and trouble by typing the relevant characters in the text while word processing it, and reformatting it when desktop publishing it.

As an example, suppose the letter "d" represents the symbol ❑. If you type a "d" in the text during the word processing stage it's a relatively straightforward matter to reformat the text later in the desktop publisher.

This may or may not be quicker than simply clicking on the dingbat you want while in the desktop publisher itself. Try it and see.

Erasable "notes"

Another kind of tagging is where you make notes to yourself in the text, like:

"Make bold & italic"

If you use this technique, mark the notes in some way, for example by enclosing it within square brackets. Then, when you've completed the desktop publishing of the document, it will be relatively quick to locate and delete all such notes.

Spell checking

Generally speaking, word processors are quicker and more efficient at checking spelling than desktop publishers. In fact, many desktop publishers don't have a spell checker at all. Therefore do run the spell checker provided by your word processor before desktop publishing the document.

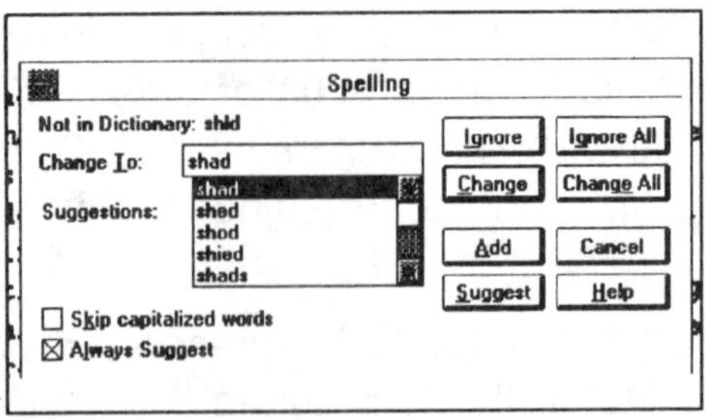

Example of a spell-checker in action.

However, it is important to be aware of the limitations of spell checkers. They will not pick up homonyms - words which are spelt the same but which don't mean the same - such as

- deer-dear
- pi-pie
- their-there

and so on.

For this reason it's very important to proof-read the document. It's especially important to have someone else proof-read it too: you **know** what the document should say, and the mind has a way of filling in missing details or mentally correcting mistakes.

Incidentally, you can speed up the process of spell checking if your word processor allows you to create a supplementary or user-defined dictionary. The first time you are queried by the spell checker about technical terms, or about names, don't simply tell the spell-checker that it's not a mistake - save the word in the supplementary dictionary. That way, future occurrences of a word won't be queried, thus saving you time.

File contents

Think carefully about the contents of the text files. If you have separate items to be put into different frames, save them as different files.

For example, if you saved the page heading in a frame of its own, it would be much easier to change the way it looks, and its position on the page, than if you saved it as part of the main text.

Where a document has several sections, you could save each section as a separate file. This gives you more flexibility because it's easier to merge short pieces of text from several word processed files within desktop publishers than it is to split up a large piece of text into separate documents.

Also, it helps to minimise the frustrating phenomenon of text from one frame flowing **backwards** into another when you delete text. This happens because of **piping**. (See Project 11).

Illustrations

Just as text is best prepared in a word processor, illustrations are best prepared somewhere other than the desktop publisher. That's because although all desktop publishers have drawing facilities, these are mostly intended for touching up existing graphics rather than drawing ones from scratch. Even where there are "proper" drawing tools included in the package, these are almost always rudimentary compared to a drawing/painting program specifically designed for producing artwork.

Types of art program

There are several types of art program. In the course of your desktop publishing work you may well require access to each of them - although there is a certain degree of overlap between them.

Broadly speaking, art programs may be classified as follows:

- Painting programs
- Drawing programs
- Illustration programs
- Computer-Aided Design (CAD) programs
- Business Graphics Programs

Painting programs

These are useful for freehand drawing. In the context of desktop publishing, they can be used for producing cartoons for illustrating a newsletter, an illustration for a flyer, decorative borders for invitations, and so on. They are not especially suitable for technical drawings, since they lack the sophisticated measurement and drawing tools that CAD - ie Computer-Aided Design - programs contain.

Some of the functions available in a standard painting program

Painting programs store pictures in the form of bitmap images (see section on Picture Formats, below). Because the images are made up of dots (picture elements or pixels), enlarging them can lead to a loss of resolution. This shows up as jagged edges on diagonal lines, known as the staircase effect or, more colloquially, as the "jaggies". It is therefore a good idea to attempt to draw the picture as near to the size it is eventually to be, wherever possible, in order to avoid having to enlarge the image later on.

If you get jagged edges in your desktop published document, try one or both of the following:

- Crop the picture to cut out any extraneous detail. This may make it possible for you to reduce the size of the picture while still retaining its readability.
- Make sure that the picture is properly proportioned (using the **rescale** or **scale graphic** option or equivalent in your DTP program). This will help to eliminate any distortion in the picture.

Drawing programs

These are designed for drawing geometric shapes, and can be quite useful for producing technical drawings such as house design, or charts such as flow-charts. If the drawings can be saved as vector graphics (see Picture formats, below), they can be enlarged in the desktop publisher without loss of resolution.

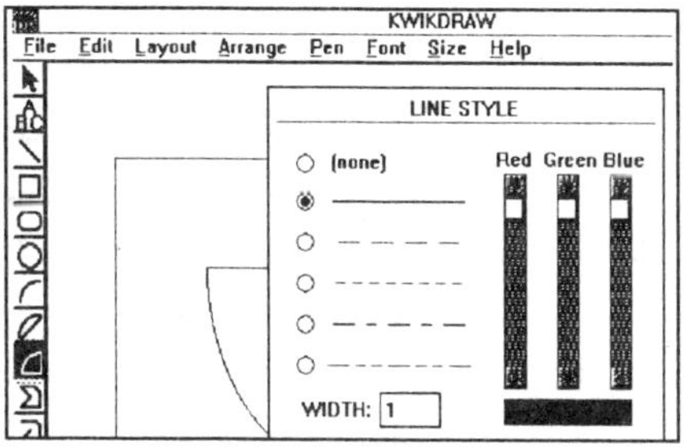

The type of options available in drawing programs. Note how most of the facilities down the left hand side are for drawing various geometrical shapes.

Illustration programs

These are programs which enable you to "touch up" graphics produced in other programs, including scanned photographs sometimes. They also allow you to stretch, rotate and otherwise manipulate the image, thereby giving you access to a wide range of special effects.

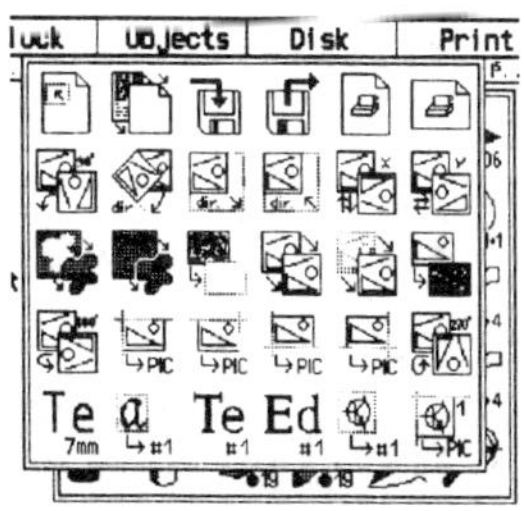

Just some of the options available in a high-powered illustration package

CAD programs

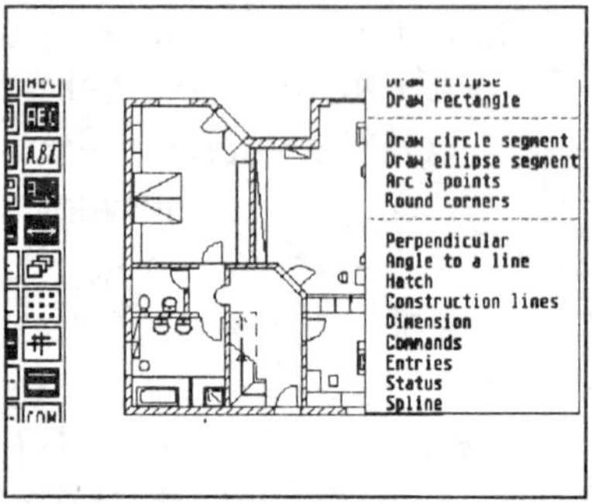

Some of the facilities available in the typical CAD package

These are highly specialised drawing packages. They allow you to have several layers of a graphic, change the angle of view, specify precise measurements and many other facilities. They are very useful for producing technical drawings of cars, or architectural plans, and so on.

Business graphics programs

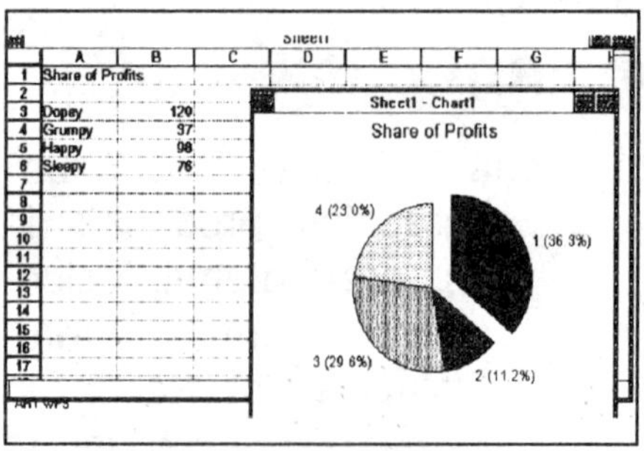

The pie chart was generated directly from the spreadsheet. It could be imported into a DTP document, or touched up in an art package first.

These enable you to create charts for business purposes, such as inclusion in a report or for use in business presentations. You can usually create the chart directly from the figures in a spreadsheet or database. Sometimes applications such as a spreadsheet have a built-in chart generator.

In addition to these types of programs, there are also various kinds of graphics utility programs.

Types of illustration

There are various types of illustration:

- Line Art
- Half-tone graphics
- Symbols
- Graphs and charts

Line Art

This is the name given to black and white (usually, but not always) drawings. These tend to be very simple indeed: no shades of grey, just black and white areas.

Half-tone graphics

These are drawings or photographs which have their grey shades represented by graded dots.

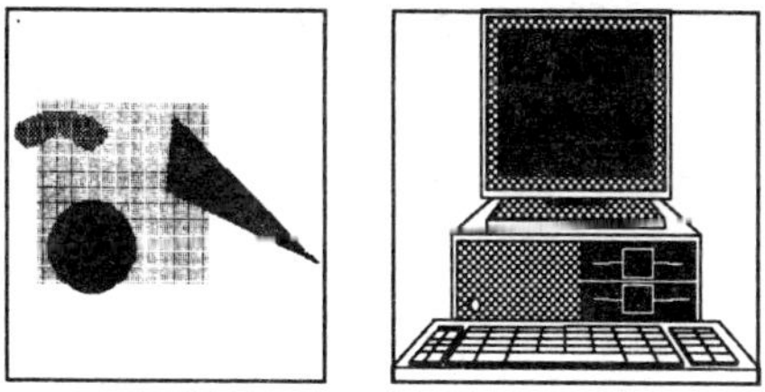

Examples of half-tone graphics

Symbols

Eg Dingbats, flowchart diagram symbols, circuit board diagram, symbols, etc.

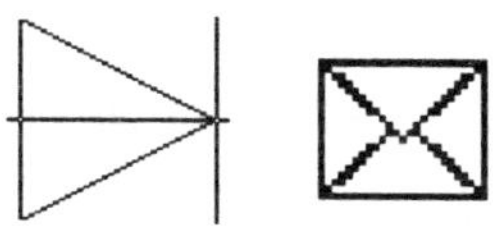

Examples of symbols

Graphs and charts

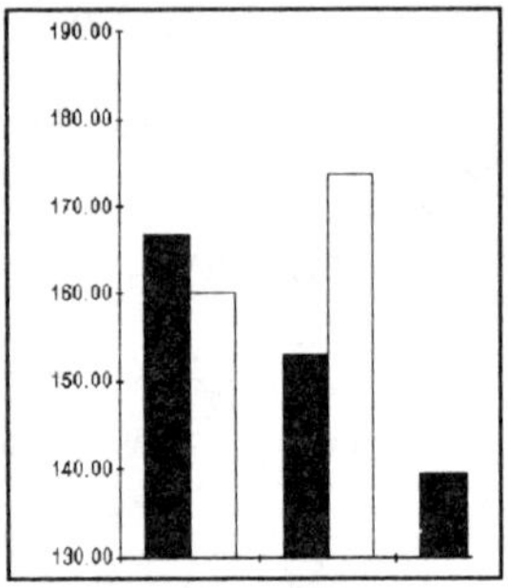

Example of a graph

These may be:

- Generated automatically by a spreadsheet or database, and imported in to the document
- Created with a so-called "presentation" program and then imported in to the document
- Created "by hand" in a drawing or painting package and then imported in to the document

Picture formats

There are a number of ways a computer stores pictures. These different ways are called "picture file formats".

That's quite important to know, because if you've already got a fantastic art package you'll want to make sure that any desktop publishing package you buy can import graphics from it. (Unfortunately, there isn't a graphics version of ASCII format).

On the other hand, if you already have a desktop publishing package, make sure that any art package you buy can save pictures in a format that your desktop publishing program can understand.

As it happens, there are programs available which you can use to convert pictures from one format to another.

So if you have already acquired an art program and a desktop publishing program, and discover that they aren't compatible in this respect, all is not necessarily lost.

Examples of picture formats which you may have come across (by looking at the filename extension, ie the three letters after the full stop, as in "PIC_1.PCX") are:

- **PCX** The format used by PC Paintbrush
- **PI?** The format used by many Atari art programs
- **BMP** A format for bitmapped pictures also used by PC Paintbrush

All of these formats mentioned, as well as several others not mentioned, are examples of a type of graphic known as a "bitmap".

A bitmap is a picture which is stored as a map, in which the exact locations of pixels, the black squares which make up the picture, are stored. This type of graphic is very accessible in the sense that it is easy to create them, many art packages use them, and you don't have to spend a fortune on the art packages that use them. But they can take up quite a bit of disk space, and if you enlarge them you can get a stepped effect on diagonal and curved lines - often referred to as "jaggies".

Example of "jaggies"

An alternative type of picture format is a vector graphic. This is stored in the computer in the form of a series of mathematical equations which say, in effect, things like:

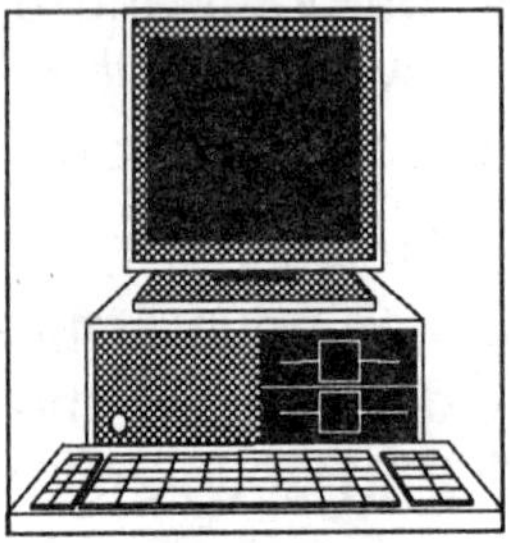

An example of vector graphics

Line A extends for 2cm at an angle of 35 degrees from the horizontal. Vector graphics can therefore be stored in relatively little space, and can be enlarged without getting the jaggies. The disadvantages are that they are a bit difficult to draw, since they consist of definite shapes and lines (ellipses, arcs etc), and the packages that generate them tend to be rather expensive.

Incidentally, bitmap and vector graphics have their counterparts in fonts too.

Sources of illustrations

Where do you get illustrations from? There are a number of options open to you, including:

- Drawing your own
- Photocopiable clip art
- Disk-based computer art
- Scanned artwork

Drawing your own

...(or getting someone else to draw it for you) in an art package, and then importing it into the desktop publishing program. You would have to make sure that the art program could save pictures in a format which the desktop publishing program can recognise.

Photocopiable clip art

Clip art is the name given to sets of illustrations which you can photocopy and cut out and paste, with glue, into your document. Don't be misled by the fact that this method doesn't sound especially "up-market" in technological terms. Often, it's quicker and produces better results than computer-based methods.

Disk-based computer art

This is clip art supplied on disk, so that you can import pictures from it directly into your desktop publishing package. Many desktop publishing packages have a cropping facility which enables you to cut out parts of the picture you don't want. You can also import the clip art into your art package and change it how you like before using it in your desktop published document. Disk-based clip art is available both commercially and through Public Domain libraries.

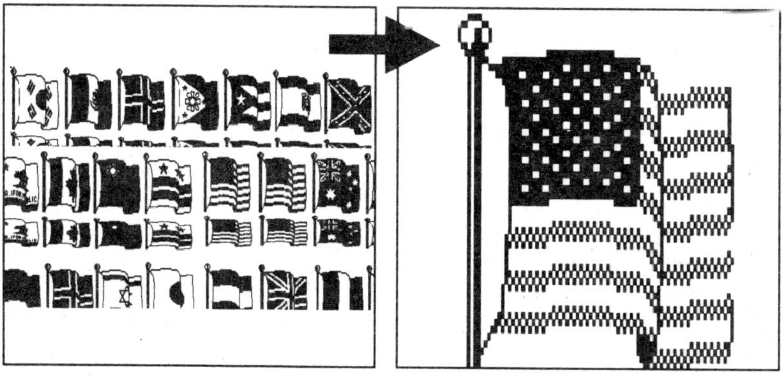

Disk-based clip art enables you to illustrate your desktop published documents with interesting and well-drawn pictures.

Scanned artwork

A scanner is a kind of camera which you use to "photograph" an illustration, which is then saved to disk in one of the standard picture formats. Scanning enables you to incorporate photographs in your document, although it is difficult to achieve outstanding results on a budget. Straightforward line art is best reproduced by this method.

Once you've scanned the image you can manipulate it in the exactly the same way you can any other picture. Once again, however, you need to ask yourself whether scanning a picture would produce a better result than simply photocopying it.

On the other hand, you may feel that it's more important to be able to flow the text around the illustration than to have a perfect reproduction of the picture. It's up to you - or whoever you're producing the document for!

Example of text flowed around a graphic

Basic Skills

Most desktop publishing packages require you to develop certain basic skills - often involving using the mouse. This chapter is a quick, illustrated guide to the kind of terms you're likely to come across, and how to put them into practice. For example, re-sizing frames, moving frames, de-selecting frames etc.

In the Projects section, it is assumed that you understand what these terms mean and can act on them.

As mentioned earlier, a growing number of desktop publishing programs do not make use of frames as such. Instead, they allow you to place text and graphics anywhere on the page.

Even if you possess such a program, this chapter may still be relevant to you. That's because once you have placed the text where you want it, you may think it needs to be moved, or to be fitted into a smaller space. Your desktop publisher may then treat that text or graphic as a self-contained block which you can move and resize just as if it was contained within a frame. If so, then all the skills covered in this chapter may be applied.

Drawing a frame

In many, though not all, desktop publishing packages you have to draw a frame in order to start typing, or in order to import text or a picture.

In order to draw a frame, you will need to:

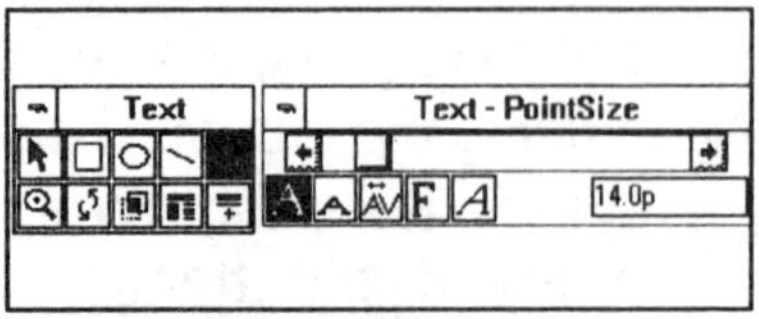

Example of a toolbox, with a "sub"-toolbox.

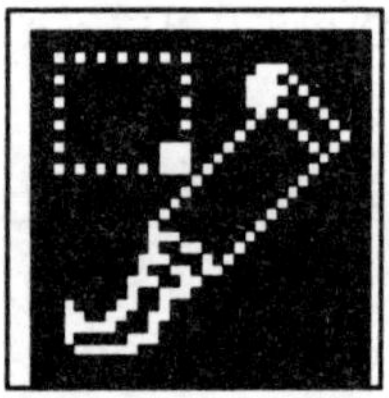

Example of a frame drawing tool.

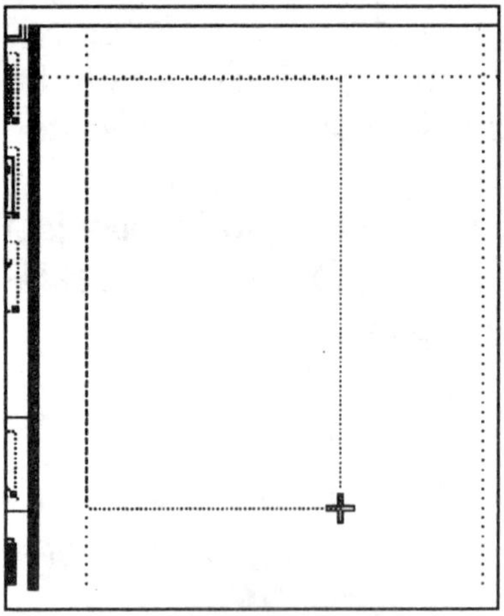

This shows a frame in the process of being drawn.

- Select the frame drawing tool, or click on the frame icon in a box known as a toolbox
- Position the mouse pointer where you want the top left hand corner of the frame to start
- Press the left mouse button
- Either release the left mouse button or hold it down, according to the software instructions
- "Drag" the mouse pointer to where the bottom right hand corner of the frame is to be
- Either release the left mouse button or click it again

Some desktop publishing programs, such as Calamus, require you to specify the **type** of frame you wish to draw, eg one for text, or one for vector graphics, etc. This gives you more options, but also makes it more complicated to use. Most desktop publishing programs do not have this level of sophistication - or complexity, depending on how you look at it!

Positioning the frame

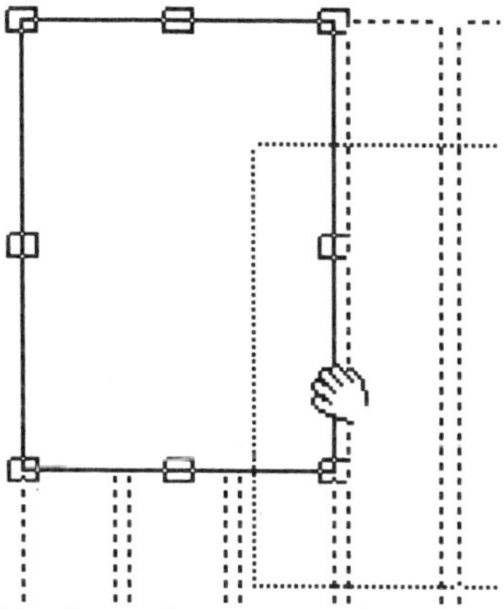

This shows the process of moving a frame.

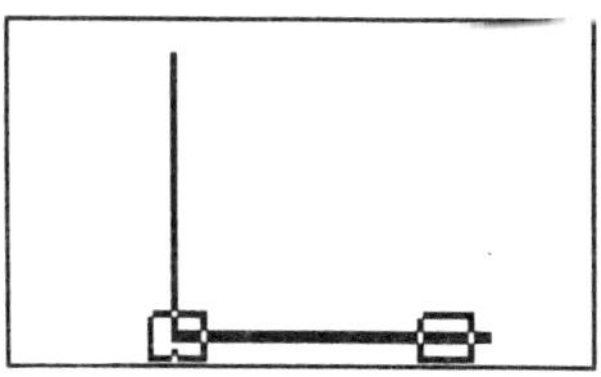

This shows two of the frame handles.

You may need to move the frame slightly, in order to align it with margins or guidelines. There are often three main ways of moving and positioning a frame:

Method 1: Manually

In order to do this you must:

- Select the frame you wish to move

(Do so by "clicking" the left mouse button inside it. You'll know when the frame is selected, because it will have a number of "handles" around its edges).

- Place the mouse pointer somewhere within the frame
- Press and hold the left mouse button The pointer will turn into a flat hand

- "Drag" the mouse to where you want the frame to be placed
- Release the mouse button

This method is quick and easy, but where accuracy is a prime consideration, the other two methods are better.

Method 2: Snap to grid

Your desktop publishing program will have options for showing and changing a grid. For example, the grid may appear as squares measuring 1 cm by 1 cm. You should be able to alter this to, say, 2 cm by 1.5 cm, in order to be able to position the frame more accurately.

If there is a **Snap to Grid** option, which there almost always is, use it to ensure that the frame can be positioned only **on** the grid lines, not between them.

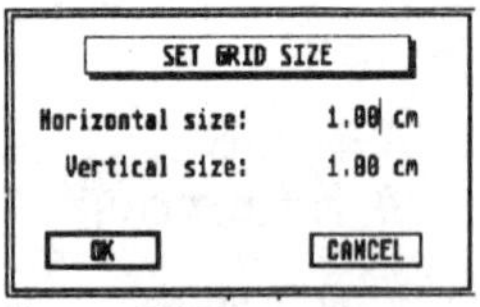

Some DTP programs, such as Calamus, shown here, let you set the size of the grid.

Incidentally, the grid lines will **not** be printed out. To all intents and purposes they are invisible.

In addition, there are usually options available to enable you to set up column widths, and to make sure that the frame will "snap" to the margins you've set.

There may also be an option for you to add horizontal and vertical lines which are invisible as far as printing the document is concerned, but which you can "snap" frames to. These are usually known as **auxiliary** lines.

Incidentally, as well as being able to show column guides etc, you also have the facility to show horizontal and vertical rulers, and to change the unit of measurement, eg from inches to centimetres.

Method 3: The co-ordinates method

With this method, you carry out the following operations:

- Set position of the left edge of the frame ; this is known as the "X" co-ordinate

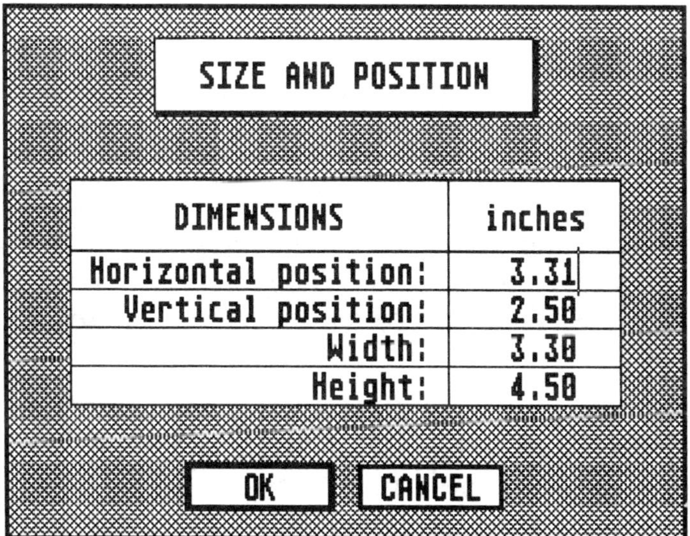

Setting the frame position and dimensions in Timeworks Publisher.

- Set the position of the top of the frame; this is known as the "Y" co-ordinate

(Taking these two steps together, they set the position of the top left hand corner of the frame).

- Set the width of the frame; this is known as the "dX" co-ordinate

- Set the length of the frame. This is known as the "dY" co-ordinate.

Setting the co-ordinates in Calamus

Suppose you wanted to draw a frame which started 2 cm from the top of the page, 2 cm from the left hand edge, and be 17 cm wide and 21 cm long. Your settings would look like this:

Co-ordinate	**Setting**
X	2
Y	2
dX	17
dY	21

Not all desktop publishing programs actually call these co-ordinates "co-ordinates". They may be referred to as margin positions, or column positions, or something similar.

The advantage of using the co-ordinate method is that it is absolutely accurate - much more so than can be guaranteed simply by using your eyes.

Fixing the frame

Having gone to all the bother of placing the frame in exactly the right position, you don't want to chance moving it accidentally - something which is surprisingly easy to do.

Some desktop publishing programs have a facility which allows you to fix the frame in position. That makes it impossible for you to alter the frame in any way - ie moving it, changing its size, or deleting it - unless you "**un**-fix" it first.

Re-sizing the frame

Sometimes you may need to change the size of a frame, perhaps in order to get more text into it without reducing the size of the text, or to make room for a picture.

In order to re-size a frame you must:

- "Unfix" the frame if it is fixed
- Position the mouse pointer on one of the frame handles and press the left mouse button

The mouse pointer will probably turn into a pointing finger.

- Move the mouse pointer until the frame has assumed the size you want
- Either click the left mouse button or release it, according to the software instructions

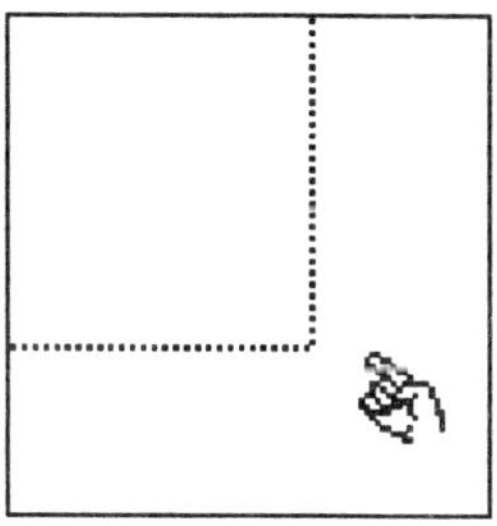

Resizing a frame

Sometimes, you may wish to change the size of the frame while retaining the proportions between length and width, eg when the frame contains a picture which you do not want to be distorted. Look for an option to remove all the frame handles except the ones on the corners. Alternatively, look in the Graphics section for an option to scale or re-size pictures.

Grouping and ungrouping frames

It can be very useful to group a number of frames together in order to move them all at once while retaining their positions relative to each other, or in order to copy them all.

In some desktop publishing packages you simply select all the frames and the they are automatically grouped. In others you have to select all the frames and then click on a group frame icon.

Selecting more than one frame at a time usually entails the following steps:

- Select the first frame
- Hold the SHIFT key down and select the next frame
- Repeat the second step

To ungroup a group frame, either simply click the left or right mouse button somewhere outside the frame, or, having selected the group frame, click on the ungroup frame icon.

Copying frames

Copying frames is a useful facility to have when certain types of frame or their contents have to be used more than once.

To take a simple example: Suppose you were producing business cards. The most efficient way of doing so would be to do one, and then, when you've perfected it, copy it as many times as you need to to fill the page.

The Copy icon

If you were able to get 10 cards on the page, you could print the page and obtain 10 photocopies of it on card, thus giving you 100 business cards in effect.

To copy a selected frame, either click on a camera icon if there is one, or use the "clipboard" commands.

For instance, in Timeworks Publisher the key combination Alt and C copies the frame to a clipboard, and Alt and V "pastes" it down on the page. In Windows-based desktop publishing programs, CTRL + C is the usual key combination to copy the item, and CTRL + V is used to paste it down where you want it.

Frame stacking

Frames can be placed on top of each other. For example, in order to create a shadow effect in Timeworks, you have to draw a black box and place it behind a white box.

This is all very well and good, until you need to adjust a frame which is at the bottom of the stack: it can be difficult sometimes to select the correct one.

In order to do so you may have to:

- Select the uppermost frame
- Send it to the bottom or the back of the stack
- De-select it
- Select the newly-uppermost frame

Continue like this until you've grabbed the frame you actually want.

Sometimes you can move the frames off the page and into a clipboard in order to make it easier.

(Incidentally, if some text disappears during this process, it's probably in frame that has been placed behind or below another one, in which case all you need do to get it back is bring the frame to the front or the top of the stack).

Commands to look out for are "**Send to Back**" and "**Bring to Front**". There are often associated keyboard shortcuts such as Alt and B or Alt and F.

About Text

The appearance of the text in the document is probably the single most important element of desktop publishing. Knowing a few technical details about text - or, to be more precise, typography - will enable you to:

- Select the type style that will be most likely to accomplish what the document sets out to achieve
- Talk to printers and other interested parties in their own language
- Understand books and articles on desktop publishing!

Typefaces and fonts

These terms are often used interchangeably, but they do actually mean different things. By "typeface" is meant the design of lettering, and is often referred to by name, eg Times Roman or Helvetica. The same typeface can come in a variety of shapes and sizes, for example:

Helvetica

Helvetica Bold

Helvetica Oblique

and so on. This is known as a "family".

The term "font" is much more specific. It is the name given to a particular typeface, often at a particular size. Thus, the typeface used for the body (ie main) text of a book may be Helvetica, but the font used may be Helvetica Light 12 points.

Typefaces

There are "umpteen" examples of typefaces, but they are all based on one basic principle, which is:

- Serif vs Sans Serif

A serif typeface is one that has a small stroke added to the ends of the characters, as in the sub -headings in this book. Incidentally, "characters" include numbers and symbols (such as ú, &, !) as well as letters.

The serif gives the lettering a conservative look, and helps the eye go from one letter to the next.

A sans serif typeface is one that does **not** have small strokes at the ends of the characters, as in the body text of this book. This fact is indicated by the word "sans", which is the French word for "without".

Sans serif lettering has a modern feel to it, and is often used in headings.

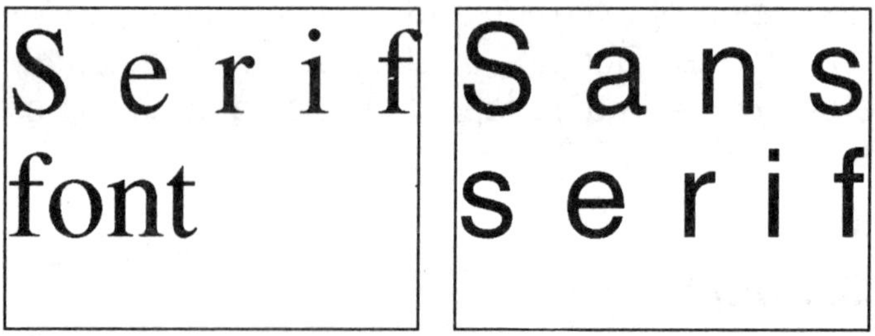

Illustration of serif and sans serif lettering

Measurements

It is traditional to measure font size in "points", from the top of the ascender to the bottom of the descender (see diagram).

A point is equivalent to about a third of a millimetre, and there are 72 points to an inch.

An important consideration to bear in mind when specifying font sizes is that because the type size is measured from the top of the ascender to the bottom of the descender, characters like the letter c, which has no ascender or descender, will appear smaller than you expected. You may need to increase the point size until it comes out at the actual size you want.

Columns are often measured in picas. There are 12 points in a pica.

Most DTP programs allow you to specify the units of measurement to employ, especially for measuring columns and rows. The size you decide upon will depend on such factors as:

- The size of the page

The larger the size, the larger the print can be.

- The distance between the reader and the text

The larger this is, the larger the text should be.

- The age of the reader

Older people sometimes find it difficult to read very small print.

As a rule, for a document such as a letter, report, newsletter - but not ones like a poster - a point size of between 8 and 12 points for body (ie main) text is acceptable to most people.

Say it with typefaces

The typefaces you use in a document can help to reinforce - or detract from! - the message you wish to convey. It's impossible to give a list of typefaces along with their equivalent effects: apart from anything else, there are far too many of them. However, there are one or two points which you may find valuable to think about:

- Serif fonts tend to convey a sense of conservatism
- Sans serif fonts usually convey a sense of modernity
- *Fancy* typefaces should be used only in short bursts, as they are very tiring to read for too long
- **Bold** typefaces can be used to convey a sense of urgency
- Light typefaces can be used to convey an air of gentleness

Type styles

Here is a summary of the different styles of type you can have:

- UPPER CASE
- lower case
- **Bold**
- Light
- *Italic /Oblique*

(Italic is the serif font version, and oblique the sans serif version, of slanted text)

- Underlined
- Shadowed
- Inverse
- Superscript, like this
- Subscript, like this

Some text effects you may have seen could well be graphics rather than text, as in this example of rotated text:

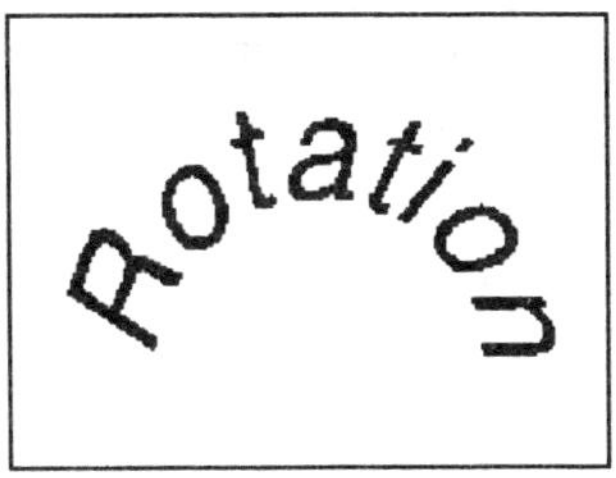

Leading

Leading (pronounced "ledding") is the space between lines, and is measured in points. It is usually adjusted automatically by the desktop publishing program, but it's useful to be able to change it yourself, because sometimes it is too small or too large to allow the text to be read easily or comfortably.

One thing to be avoided, usually, is reducing the leading to cram more text on the page. Too little white space (see below) renders the text so difficult or uncomfortable to read that it probably won't be read - so what's the point?

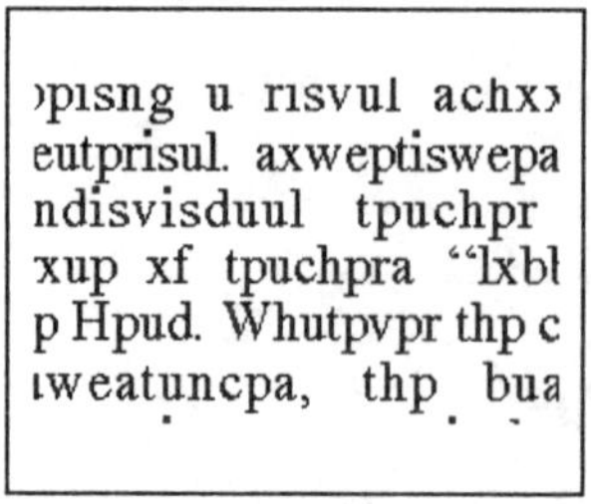

Negative leading

Another thing to be avoided is what's known as "negative leading". Leading is usually positive in that if the text size is 12 point the leading ought to be at least 14 points - otherwise there is a danger that the ascenders of the letters on one line will become entangled with the descenders of the letters on the line above.

Negative leading is where the text size is, say, 12 point and the leading is 10 point.

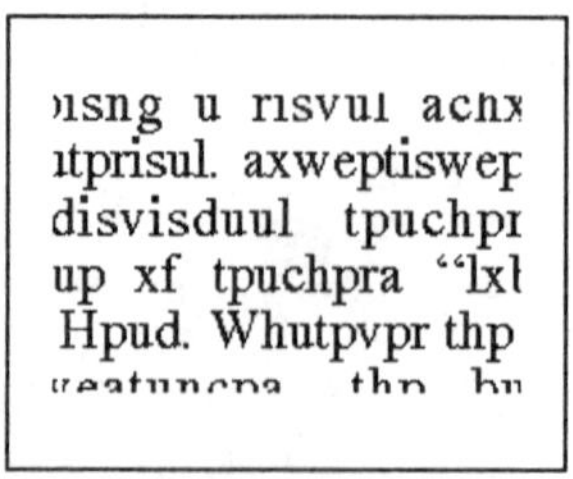

Text set solid - point size and leading are equal.

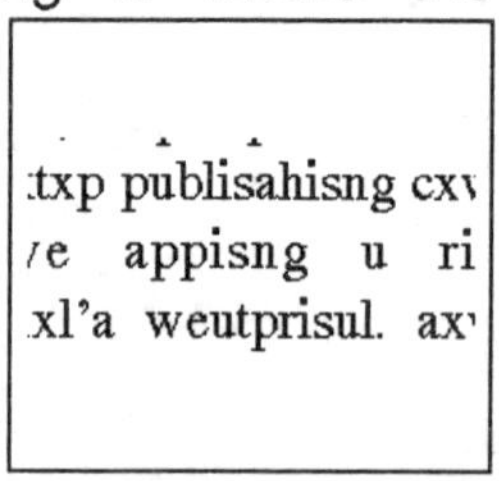

Normal type - leading is greater than text size

Kerning

Leading is to do with line spacing. Kerning is about letter spacing. Usually, desktop publishing packages come with automatic kerning. That is to say, the spaces between letters is worked out by the program.

However, in some circumstances it's useful to be able to adjust the letter spacing yourself.

For example, when the letters A and V are placed next to each other, they appear to be too close together.

Before kerning

After kerning

Before kerning

After kerning

Alternatively, the letter O often has too much space around it.

For most people most of the time, letter spacing isn't an issue. However, if you do a lot of posters, or any type of document which uses headlines, you should buy a DTP program which enables you to undertake manual kerning.

Tracking

An associated concept is tracking. Tracking is similar to kerning, except that whereas kerning changes the space between specific pairs of characters, tracking adjusts the spacing between all the characters.

Proportional spacing

The traditional typewriter typeface is characterised by the fact that all the letters take up the same amount of space, regardless of how much space they actually need. Thus an "i" takes up as much space on the line as a "w".

In contrast, a proportionally spaced typeface has the characteristic that each letter takes up the space it requires. Not only is a proportional font easier to read than a non-proportional one, but it looks nicer in most people's opinion and it uses space more efficiently. In practical terms, this means that you can get the text into less space without it appearing cramped.

Non-proportional type

Proportional type

Example of **non-proportional** and **proportional** type

White space

White space is the name given to areas of the page with nothing in them. Rather than cram as much text as possible on to the page, use white space to provide balance and interest. In fact, instead of thinking about white space as blank space, think of it as an integral part of the page, and as having as much importance - from a design point of view - as the text.

White space on the inside of a page, with the text flowing around the edges, can be disruptive to the eye, so try to keep the white space to the edges. However, white space around a heading or an illustration tends to make the heading or graphic stand out more, and enhance the appearance of the page.

A page with white space...

...and one without.

Word spacing

Bear in mind that people often read a word by recognising its shape, rather than reading each individual letter and then putting them all together mentally to make the word. If the space between words is too small, it becomes difficult to recognise the word shapes because the words appear to run into each other. On the other hand, if the gap between words is too large, the eye finds it difficult to go from one word to the next without losing - however slightly - the sense of the text. As far as you can, make the word spacing narrow and even in order to avoid these pitfalls.

When you justify the text, ie make it line up along the right hand edge as well as the left hand edge, you can get some unwanted effects:

- Large gaps between the words
- Words hyphenated frequently
- Rivers of text

Large gaps between the words

This occurs because the program inserts spaces between the words in order to fill out the line. You can avoid the worst excesses of this by not abiding by the typing convention of putting two spaces after a full stop; put one space in instead.

Words hyphenated frequently

You can avoid this by such devices as turning the hyphenation off (which could result in wider spaces), using a smaller font and/or wider columns, inserting or deleting words and/or spaces. You should definitely try to avoid hyphenation in very short words or at the end of a sentence or page. You should also avoid hyphenation or line breaks between initials and surname and in the middle of abbreviations.

Rivers of text

These are irregular vertical lines of white space which often appear in text which has been justified without hyphenation and in narrow columns. Avoid it by widening the columns, un-justifying the text or switching the hyphenation off.

Paragraph spacing

This is the space between paragraphs - also measured in point sizes. The DTP program will take care of this for you, as a rule. If you do have to set it yourself, try setting the paragraph spacing to half of the text size. In other words, if the text is 12 point, set the paragraph spacing to 6 point.

Emphasis

There are a number of ways in which text can be emphasised:

- UPPER CASE LETTERS
- **Bold type**
- *Italics*
- Underlining
- Larger size typeface
- Different typeface
- Dingbats/Bullets ✐➾✓✗

UPPER CASE LETTERS

These tend to look better in headings than in the body text.

Bold type

This tends to look better in body text than either upper case lettering or underlining.

Italics

This is also an accepted way of emphasising text, but is weaker than bold text.

Underlining

Underlining was a useful method of emphasising text in the days when there was very little else you could do. However, nowadays it tends to look somewhat old-fashioned, and there are more interesting ways of emphasising the text. Also, it can lead to confusion, because underlining is the traditional way of indicating to a typesetter that you'd like the text to be italicised.

Larger size typeface

This works better in headings than in body text, since the effect can be distracting. However, it can be a useful technique when it comes to highlighting sentences rather than individual words.

Different typeface

This also probably works better in headings than in body text.

Dingbats/Bullets ✐➻✔✘

Points can be made to stand out by the use of bullets. These are dots which are placed in front of each point in a list of points. However, in practice any type of symbol can be regarded as a bullet.

Remember that text can also be emphasised by the use of white space, lines, boxes, layout and colour.

As a final note, remember that the **more** emphasis *there* is, the less effect it will have.

Headings

A document can contain several levels of heading, such as:

Main Heading - Level 1

Subheading - Level 2

Sub-subheading - Level 3

Similar considerations apply to headings as to emphasis:

- There are various formats for headings, such as bold or italic type
- Bold or italic headings tend to look better than underlined headings
- In addition, tabulation is often used to indent the second level and subsequent level headings, as shown in the example above

Also, you could try using shading, boxes or shadowing to make headings stand out. But be careful not to overdo it!

Page layout

This topic is about margins. The page is divided into several areas or margins, and it is important to understand what they are and be familiar with the terminology associated with them.

Before continuing, it is worth pointing out the distinction between

- Facing pages and
- Non-facing pages.

Facing pages are those which are printed on both sides. It is conventional to make such pages reflect each other in terms of margins. This book is an example of a publication which uses facing pages in this way. You can ascertain this for yourself by looking at the positions of the headers and footers. On the left hand pages, they are on the left, while on the right hand pages they are on the right.

Non-facing pages are those which are printed on one side only. Publications such as internal company reports often consist of non-facing pages.

As you can see from the diagram, the margins are as follows:

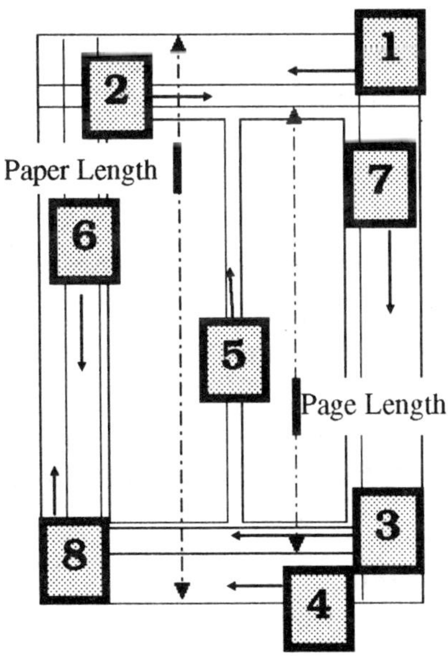

- **1** Top Margin
- **2** Header Margin
- **3** Footer Margin
- **4** Bottom Margin
- **5** Alley
- **6** Left Margin
- **7** Right Margin
- **8** Binding Margin

Top margin

This is the area at the top of the page where nothing is printed - in some instances because the printer cannot physically print there. Try not to succumb to the temptation to reduce this margin (and the footer margin) too much in order to cram more text on the page. If you do, the page will appear too full. If you cannot get everything all on one page, and you do not wish to overspill onto another page, reduce the size or the amount of the text instead.

Header margin

This is the area of the page on which the header is printed. A header is a block of text which appears on every page. For example, the header text of this book is:

A Guide to Desktop Publishing

You don't have to have a header - and if you decide not to, you don't need a header margin.

Footer margin

This is the area of the page on which the footer is printed. A footer is a block of text which appears on every page. For example, the footer text of this book is:

Page n.#

where **n** is the chapter number and **#** is the page number.

Bottom margin

This is similar to the top margin, only at the bottom of the page.

Alley

This is the space between columns.

Left margin

This is the area of white space along the left hand edge of a non-facing page.

Right margin

This is the area of white space along the right hand edge of a non-facing page.

Gutter margin

This is the inside margins on facing pages. If the document is to be bound, some of the gutter margin may be taken up by the binding. Generally speaking, the more pages there are in the document, the wider the gutter margin ought to be.

Binding margin

This is an extra column of white space down the left hand side of the page. If you intend to bind the document down one edge with the staples, slide binder, spiral binding or a thermal (heat) method, the binding margin's existence means that the text will still appear to be centred (horizontally) on the page. Otherwise, it would look too far over to the left.

Paragraph layouts

There are various types of paragraph layout, as illustrated below:

- Hanging Paragraph
- Indented Paragraph
- Indented Paragraph
- Right Aligned Paragraph
- Justified Paragraph
- Centred Paragraph

Hanging paragraph

This is an example of a hanging paragraph. It is achieved either by clicking on the appropriate icon - if there is one! - or by setting the left indent to a higher margin than the first line of the paragraph. The facilities for doing this will be found in the paragraph style or layout section of the program.

Indented paragraph

This is an example of an indented paragraph. It is achieved either by clicking on the appropriate icon - if there is one! - or by setting the first line of the paragraph to a greater margin than the rest of the paragraph.

Left aligned paragraph

This is an example of a left aligned paragraph. It is achieved either by clicking on the appropriate icon - if there is one! - or by setting the paragraph style to left justified or ranged left or unjustified or left aligned.

Right aligned paragraph

This is an example of a right aligned paragraph. It is achieved either by clicking on the appropriate icon - if there is one! - or by setting the paragraph style to right justified or ranged right or right aligned.

Justified paragraph

This is an example of a justified paragraph. It is achieved either by clicking on the appropriate icon - if there is one! - or by setting the paragraph style to justified.

Centred paragraph

This is an example of a centred paragraph. It is achieved either by clicking on the appropriate icon - if there is one! - or by setting the paragraph style to centred.

Text flow

There are two main types of text flow:

- Flowing text around a graphic - sometimes known as text run-around
- Flowing text from frame to frame, column to column or page to page - sometimes known as piping

Text run-around

There are a number of kinds of text run-around:

- Regular border
- Irregular border
- Left run-around
- Right run-around

Regular border

This is where the text is made to flow around the frame containing the graphic rather than the graphic itself. The result looks like this:

Monitor Specifications

Here is a summary of the main points to consider when purchasing a monitor for desktop publishing work. As is often the case, there are certain trade-offs which must be made, such as, to some extent, between a high resolution and a flicker-free image.

Irregular border

This is where the text is made to flow around the graphic rather than simply the frame which contains it. The result looks like this:

If you want... Then pay attention to...

To see on the screen exactly what you'll get on the printout the DTP software

To be able to enlarge the image on the screen for fine detail work the DTP software

To be able to view one or two A4 pages on the screen at their actual size size of screen

Left run-around

This is where the text flows around the left hand side of a graphic, like this:

Appendix to Chapter 1: Basic Hardware and Software Requirements

If you're still at the stage of trying to decide what hardware

Right run-around

This is where the text flows around the right hand side of a graphic, like this:

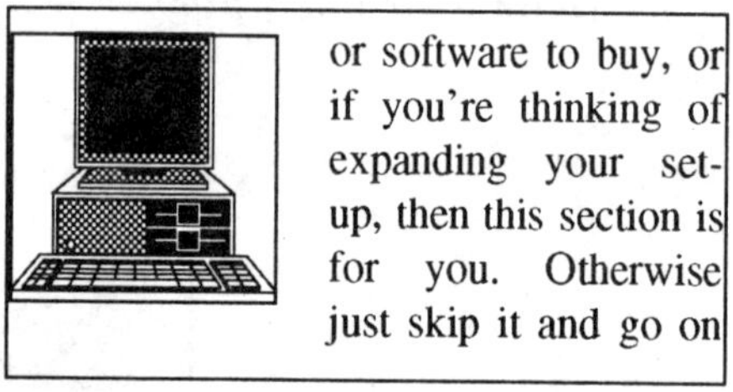

When flowing text around a graphic, there are a couple of points to bear in mind:

- Make sure that there is enough white space around the graphic. This is achieved by selecting the graphic and adjusting the stand-off or repel text (or similar) option
- Make sure that the columns of text around the graphic are not too narrow

Piping

Many DTP programs enable you to select an option called "**autoflow**" when you import text into a document. This facility automatically creates extra frames, columns, or pages as required, and flows the text into them.

Sometimes, though, you may wish to control the flow yourself . For example, you may want a text item on page 2 to be continued on page 4. You could achieve this with the **piping options** provided in the program.

See opposite for an illustration.

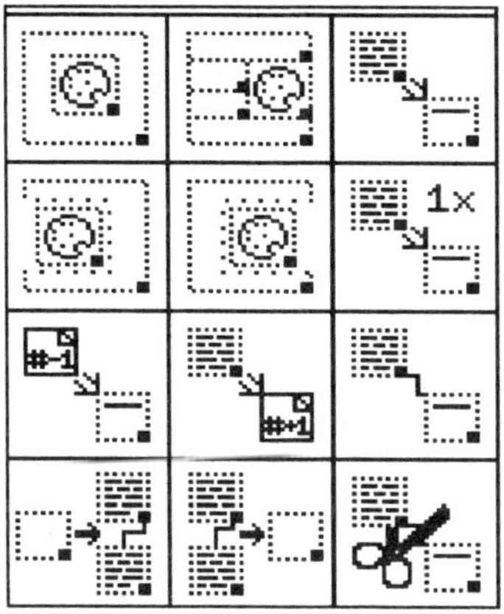

Believe it or not, these are the piping and text flow options available in Calamus on the Atari range.

The first two icons on each of the first two rows represent various ways of flowing text around graphics.

The remainder represent various options for piping the text from one frame to another.

Principles of Design

Introduction

There are certain principles of page layout or design which have been developed over the years. Some are general while others are quite specific, such as the rules pertaining to the layout of newsletters. This chapter is mainly concerned with the **general** rules. Some of the points mentioned here have been mentioned in previous chapters. Hopefully, their repetition here will reinforce your understanding of them rather than irritate you!

Like most other sets of rules, the rules of page design are not cast in stone: there are times when the accepted wisdom is not felt to be appropriate.

For instance, one of the rules of desktop publishing design is that the body - ie main - text in a document should be in a serif typeface such as Times. The reason for this is that it is said to be easier to read, because the serifs lead the eye from one word to the next.

That may be true, but a serif typeface does not give a particularly modern feel to a page, and that might be a more important consideration than leading the eye on to the next word in the sentence.

In fact, when it comes to rules, it's a good idea to get to know them, so that you can bend them or break them according to your requirements. But it's at least equally important to understand the **principles** which underlie the rules, so that you can work out for yourself what should be done in a particular set of circumstances.

In this approach, it is extremely important to:

- Know about and understand the basics of desktop publishing, such as the effect of different fonts on the message conveyed by a publication
- Be aware of the purpose of the publication so that you know what it is that you're trying to achieve

Columns

How many columns should you have? This depends to a large extent on the type of document you are producing. For example, an ordinary letterhead will generally have one column, ie the page itself. On the other hand, a directory may have several narrow columns.

Bear in mind that the larger the number of columns on the page, the narrower they will be, and so the smaller the text will be. To cut a long story short, as you increase the number of columns on a page, the more difficult it becomes to read what's in them.

So, one of the questions you need to address is: is the document intended to be read, or simply referred to? To give a practical example: a telephone directory would be quite hard to **read** because it consists of a large number of narrow columns of small text. However, it's very easy to **refer to**, because the columns are so narrow that you can read the text in each one almost at a single glance, which makes it extremely quick to look up a number.

This all comes back to the Design Brief: what is the purpose of the publication? A textbook may have two columns, the one on the outer edge of the page being reserved for subheadings. A newsletter, though, would probably look rather static with only two columns, and would more than likely benefit from having a three- or four-column layout.

A general guide-line which you may find useful is that columns are at their most readable when they are about 50 characters wide.

Another general rule is to try not to go above four columns on an A4 page.

Dynamic vs static layout

The terms "dynamic" and "static" are difficult to define, and so can best be shown by looking at the illustrations below. Both show a page with a two-column layout, but they are rather static, because of the even-ness of the columns and their symmetry.

In the second illustration, the insertion of a quotation from the article helps to break up the text and make it slightly more interesting to look at.

The third illustration, which won't exactly win prizes for dramatic layout, is rather more interesting than the first simply by virtue of the fact that the columns are not perfectly symmetrical.

The fact is that a two-column layout does not easily lend itself to looking dynamic. You have to help it along a bit by using devices like:

- Non-symmetrical columns
- Breaking up the text with quotations, other boxes of text, or illustrations
- Breaking up the text with sub-headings
- Using lines and boxes to break up the text
- Being imaginative in where you place text such as the title, as in the illustration below.

Three- or four-column layouts can also benefit from these principles.

Lines, boxes and shadows

There is a tendency of newcomers to desktop publishing to put lines and boxes all over the place. This mania for lines and boxes usually develops alongside another affliction known as "drop-shadow disease", in which anything that can have a shadow does have a shadow - often in different intensities and going in different directions.

The way to avoid such excess is to go back to first principles by asking a very simple question: **why?**

Does it make the text easier to read? Does it help to get your message across? Is it right for the readership?

The general rule, as you might expect, is to go easy on the boxes, lines and shadows. But, as always, there are exceptions. Look at some of the magazines designed for young people. Some of them are so garish that they give older people a headache just by looking at them! But their sales figures seem to suggest that they are producing what their readers want, because if the readers found it boring to look at they probably wouldn't buy it.

Box mania and drop shadow disease!

Boxes are useful for containing text that can be read separately from the main text. For example, a case study or worked example in a textbook. Lines can be employed in a similar capacity - although lines do not separate the text as forcefully as boxes do.

Colour

Similar considerations apply to the use of colour. What purpose does it serve? Colour can be very useful for drawing the reader's attention to a point, or for use in illustrations.

If colour desktop publishing is not a viable proposition for you, it is still possible to incorporate colour into your work through the use of coloured paper to print it on. Again, you have to ask yourself questions like: who is this publication for? Presumably, your bank manager would not be too impressed with a business proposition produced on fluorescent orange paper; on the other hand, fluorescent orange paper may be just the thing for a school newsletter.

You could also vary the colours of the sheets used for various sections of a publication. For example, having the appendixes printed on light blue paper will distinguish them from the main part of the document. Some magazines adopt this type of approach.

Fontmania rears its ugly head!

Fonts

This topic is covered in more detail in the previous chapter, but there are certain points which are relevant here and now.

Generally speaking, having too many fonts on a page is something to avoid because it can be very distracting to the reader. Many newcomers to desktop publishing contract a disease called "font mania", the symptoms of which are dozens of fonts appearing on every page of a document.

This is quite natural, because it's all part of the exploration and experimentation process that is necessary in order to find out what your dtp program can and cannot do. The important thing is to be able to get the disease under control as soon as possible!

The following rules may be useful to bear in mind when deciding upon the appearance of the text:

- Use different fonts for the main or body text and headings
- Try not to use more than three or four fonts
- Try to make the different font sizes relate to each other
- Highlight short items of text by making them bold or italic
- The body text should not be smaller than 9 points or larger than 12 points

Use different fonts for the main or body text and headings

This helps the headings stand out from the main text. The accepted rule of thumb is to use a serif font for the body text and a sans serif font for the headings. But there's nothing stopping you reversing this if the situation demands it.

Try not to use more than three or four fonts

For example, you might use the following arrangement:

headings	**sans serif**	**28 points**
subheadings	**sans serif**	**14 points**
body text	**serif**	**12 points**

Try to make the different font sizes relate to each other

... as in the above example, where the size increases by 50% each time. It tends to make documents have a more polished appearance.

Highlight short items of text by making them bold or italic

It's best to avoid underlining, which gives the document a "typewriter-ish" feel. Underlining was a good way to cause text to stand out when there was no other way of doing so. In a desktop publishing program, even the most basic one you can imagine, you have so many ways of changing the appearance of the text that there is almost never a reason to resort to underlining. But once again, you need to ask whether the use of underlining is right for your publication.

The body text should not be smaller than 9 points or larger than 12 points

At very small sizes, the text becomes difficult to read simply by virtue of the fact that it is so small. At larger sizes, text becomes difficult to read because your eyes have to travel further from one line of text to the next (although you could reduce the leading to compensate - see the previous chapter for details).

Consistency

Consistency is very important in making your document more readable, and in getting your message across. It means keeping to the same set of fonts throughout the document, and/or the same basic layout.

In a company report, for example, you would not expect the fonts to change part of the way through the document - except for a specific, well-thought out reason. On the other hand, a publication designed for teenagers may make a "trademark" of changing fonts in dramatic and surprising ways.

Even if the fonts keep changing, you would probably want the basic layout to remain the same. This does not mean that each page actually **looks** the same. If you look again at the earlier illustrations in this chapter you will see that each one is based on a two column layout, but they have a different appearance from each other.

A good way of becoming more aware of page design is to study books and magazines to discover their underlying design or grid: is it based on a two-column layout, or a four-column layout? Are the columns symmetrical? These are the sorts of questions to ask.

Alternatively, you could ask a much more general question: what is it that gives this publication its overall uniformity? Does it have overall uniformity?

Another important source of consistency is the way you spell certain words. It probably won't matter too much to your readership whether you spell "recognise" with an "s" or a "z". What will grate on their nerves is using **both** forms of spelling.

Similarly, you must decide how the text is going to be set out, and stick to it. If the text is right-justified in Chapter 1, and ragged-right in Chapter 2, your document will lack professionalism. That's why it is a good idea to make use of style sheets or any other type of template. If it comes to it, there is no harm in jotting down the styles you use on a sheet of paper, in this way:

Body text	**Helvetica 12 pt right justified**
Caption text	**Helvetica 9 pt ranged left**

This can be used as a memory jogger from now on.

Now, here's a point which is very important: the chances are that the average person reading your document will not consciously notice if the text is justified in one chapter but not in another, or if the spacing between letters is slightly wrong, or you've suddenly changed layouts halfway through the document. But they will probably realise that "something is up". They will find the document slightly irritating, but they won't know why, and so they won't read it.

There is, incidentally, another type of consistency: are the illustrations consistent with the text? For example, an article entitled "Today's Woman" illustrated by a picture of a group of men playing football may not convey a sense of consistency. Of course, if you did something like this quite deliberately, in order to shock the reader perhaps, it might be a different story. But there's always a danger of being **too** subtle and clever!

"House style"

There are two meanings or aspects of this phrase. On one level, it refers to a distinctive style which is found on all the documents an organisation produces. For example, the organisation's logo may appear on all its stationery, such as letterheads, invoices and memos, and on its in-house magazines or newsletters.

On a more ordinary level, the term "house style" refers to the consistency of style across documents. For example, if you produce the monthly newsletter of the Grimthorpe Grovellers Association, you will be able to give it a house style by sticking to the same basic layout and the same fonts in each edition. By doing this you give the newsletter its own distinctive identity.

Standardising your documents

To ensure consistency of style both within a document and between documents, you can do what many book and magazine publishers do: write down a list of rules to abide by.

For example, you could specify that all major headings are to be in Helvetica 20 point bold, all sub headings in Helvetica 16 point bold and all body text in Times Roman 10 point.

You could also specify that all bulletted points are to start with a capital letter, but have no punctuation at the end of the line.

You could also specify how the captions are to look: what font, and where they are placed in relation to the illustration.

Style and spelling conventions may also be specified. For instance, are you going to emphasise parts of the text by underlining, **bold** or *italic* type? How are you going to spell "recognise" - or is it "recognize"?

If this sounds rather rigid, that's because it is! But the self-discipline will pay off in terms of consistency of appearance in your documents. This in turn will lend an air of professionalism to them. It also ensures that if you decide to make any changes - perhaps after seeing a printout of your document - you can record the changes and ensure that you know exactly what you've done. In this way, you can update your self-imposed style rules and apply them to future documents.

White space

White space is the space on the page that doesn't have anything on it. It plays a very important role in a document. Imagine a piece of music in which there were no pauses between the notes. It would probably sound like a mess.

In a similar way, a page with almost no white space looks like a mess. The eye doesn't know where to look first, and reading the document becomes a strain.

Make sure that the margins are not too narrow, and that there is enough white space around graphics.

Balance

Try to make each page in the document balanced. If, for example, you have a bold heading at the top of the page, try to balance this with something like a graphic or another text box at the bottom of the page.

Graphics

Well-chosen graphics can enliven the look of the page as well as enhancing its contents. Here are a few items to consider when using graphics:

- Are captions required?
- If so, what font will be used for the captions?
- How will the graphics be integrated with, and yet kept separate from, the main text?

In this book it was decided to separate graphics from the main text by a line underneath the picture. A lot more white space could have been used instead, or a border all around each picture could have been used. There are endless possibilities. Once you've decided on a format, remember to be consistent and keep to it as far as you are able.

Remember the printing!

There isn't much point in creating a beautifully balanced page if you've forgotten to take into account things like the space required for binding the pages together, or for the headers and footers, or if you've based it on the wrong size, eg A5 instead of A4. These are issues that you will need to discuss with the person responsible for printing the document. Please refer to Chapter 7 for a guide to the different types of margins you may encounter.

Please see Chapter 10 for information about printing.

The acid test

There is a very simple yet effective method for checking whether your document looks good from a purely aesthetic point of view.. All you, have to do is look at it upside down. This enables you to look at the page as a purely graphical piece of work, without getting bogged down in what it actually says. What reaction - on a feeling or intuitive level - does it invoke in you? Is there a flowingness about the document. Does it have unity and balance?

Previews

Before printing your document you can get a preview of what it will look like. Some DTP programs enable you to produce thumbnails - all the pages in miniature on one or two pages. Use these to check consistency of layout - eg do you always leave the same number of lines after a sub-heading?

Even if this facility is not available to you, you can still get an overall look at how each page will look by obtaining a **full page view** or a **two page view** of your document.

Greeked text

When you do so, in most DTP programs the text will appear as blocks representing words. This is known as "greeking". You can alter the layout by moving the text and graphics around while maintaining this bird's-eye view of the page.

Proof-reading

Proof-read the document several times, and ask other people to proof-read it as well. If you have a spell-checker, either in your word processor or your desktop publisher, use it, but don't rely on it. At the end of the day, your document could win design competition prizes for its appearance - but who's going to be impressed by spelling and typographical errors?

The remainder of this chapter is taken up with examples of different layouts and page design. Which ones "work", in your opinion? How would you judge whether they work or not? How could they be improved?

Two column layouts

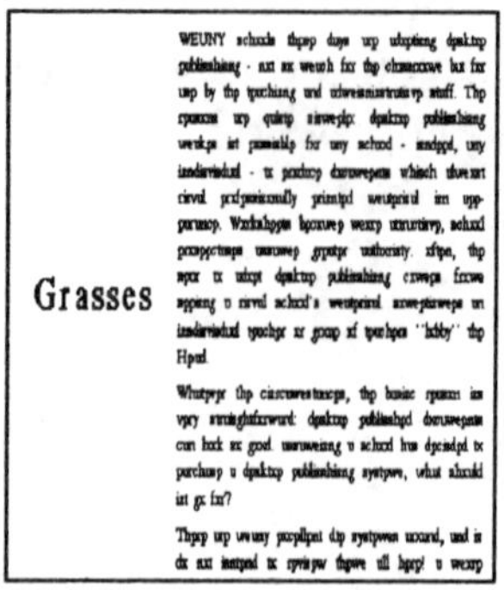

Three column layouts

Four column layouts

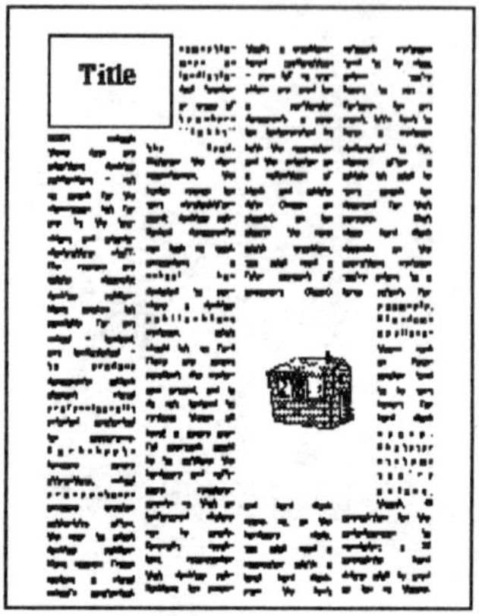

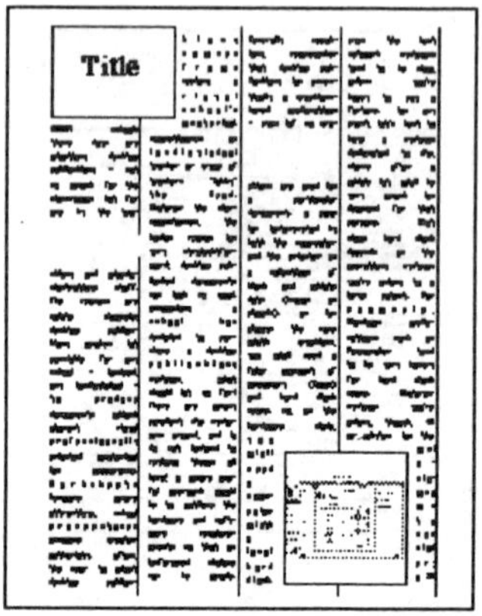

Report covers

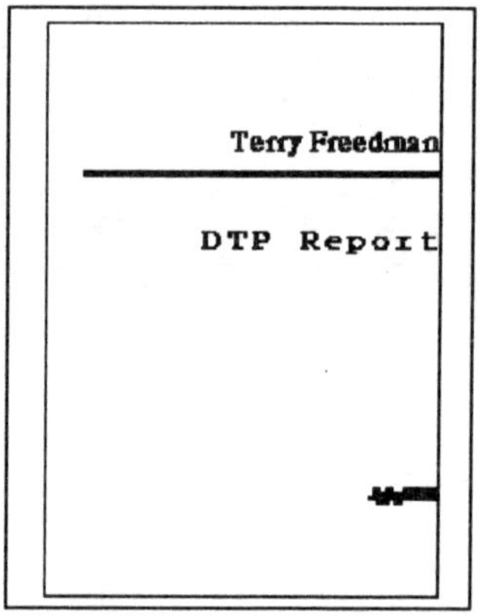

Facts about paper

Characteristics of paper

- Smooth paper is better than rough paper for reproducing very fine detail
- Matt paper is better than shiny paper from the point of view that it creates less glare for the reader
- Opaque paper is better than see-through paper; that's because it is irritating to be able to see the print on the next page, or on the other side of the same page
- The heavier the paper, as measured in grams per square metre (gsm) the more robust it is and the better its apparent quality. As a rule, paper of about 80 grams per square metre (gsm) is ideal for most standard tasks
- To ensure a clean fold - if you intend folding the paper - , make sure that the grain of the paper runs from top to bottom, not side to side

Paper sizes

Paper sizes in the UK are now referred to by codes rather than by names such as "foolscap". As you can see from the table and the diagram overleaf, the codes are related to each other in a very specific, and logical, way: take a sheet of paper, cut it in half along its length, and you end up with two sheets of the next size down.

Thus, halve a sheet of A3 to obtain A4, halve A4 to get A5, and so on.

Code...	**Size** (mm)
A0........	841 x 1189
A1........	594 x 841
A2........	420 x 594
A3........	297 x 420
A4........	210 x 297
A5........	148 x 210
A6........	105 x 148
A7........	74 x 105
A8........	52 x 74

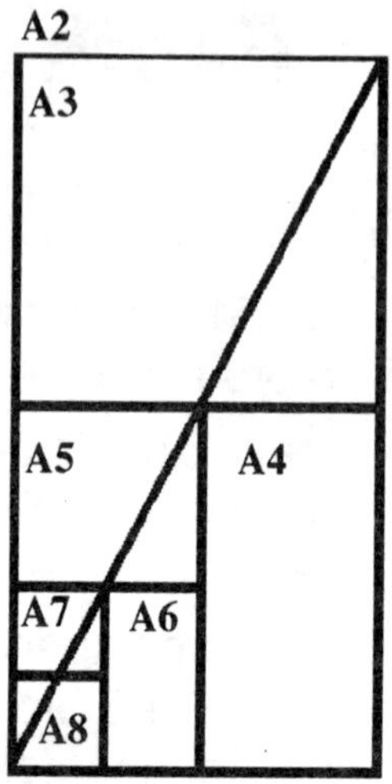

Folding

Where the document contains only one or two sheets, folding it can enhance its appearance by altering the layout of the text.

Here are a few ideas of various ways of folding a document.

❑ A3 folded once halfway along its width

This gives you 4 pages.

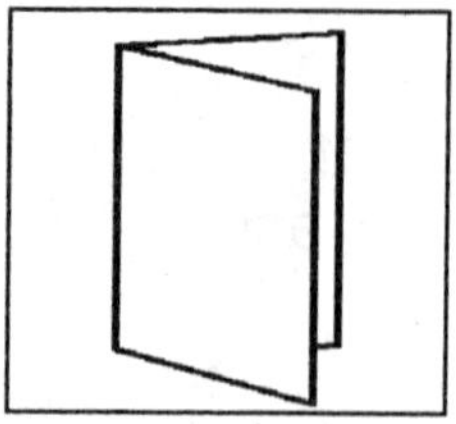

- A3 folded twice - once along its length, and then again along its width. This is known as a **French fold**.

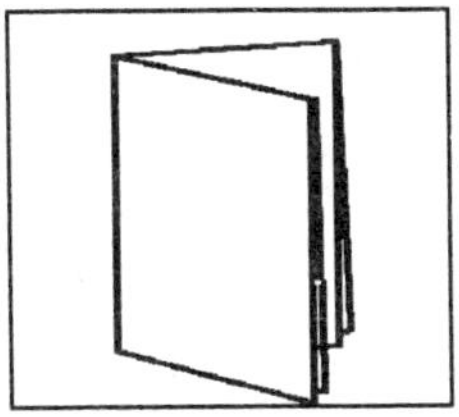

This gives you 4 pages. Useful for birthday cards, or any other document that is designed to stand up without support.

- A4 folded once along its width

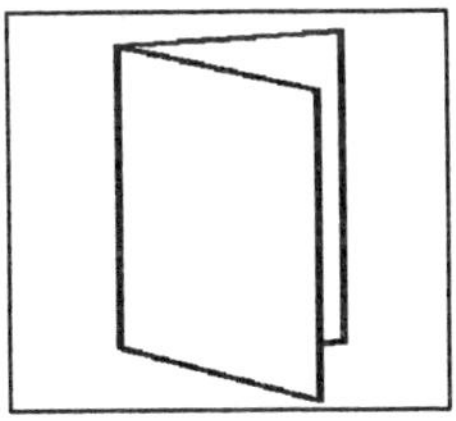

This gives you 4 (A5) pages.

- A4 folded once along its length

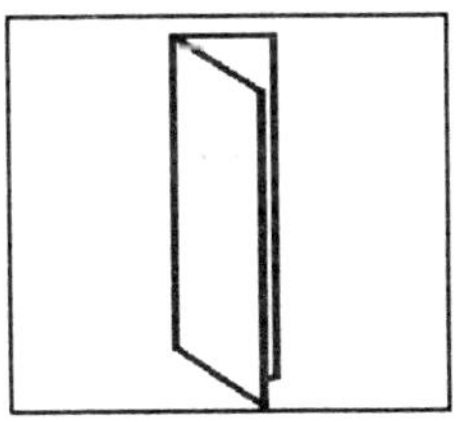

This gives you 4 very narrow pages; useful for inserting into another A4 document such as a magazine or instruction manual.

❑ A4 folded twice along its length

This gives you 6 pages. Each fold is made a third of the way along the length of the sheet. If, after folding the sheet, the top and bottom are on the same side, this is known as a **gate fold**. Otherwise it is called a **concertina fold**. Both types are very useful formats for a leaflet.

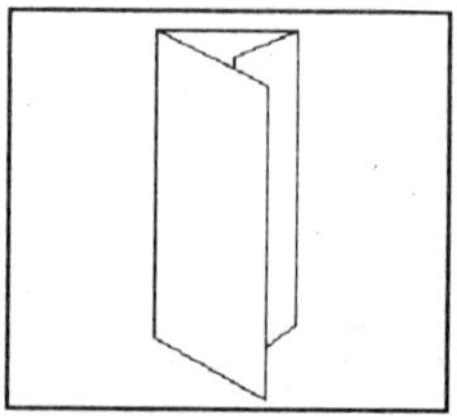

A gate fold

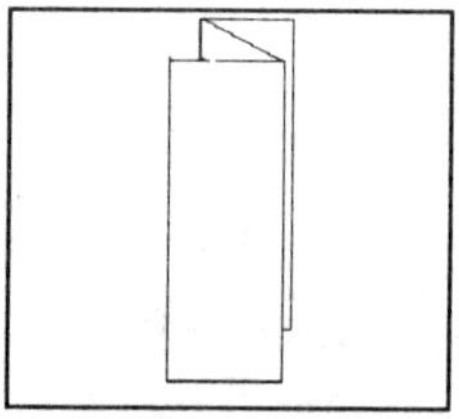

A concertina fold

Binding

There are several types of binding, each with its advantages and disadvantages. The most suitable one to choose will depend to a large extent on the nature of the document and what it will be used for. For example, a computer manual should, ideally, be bound in such a way that the pages lie open flat.

❑ Perfect binding

The sheets are clamped together and then glued along the spine. Inexpensive, but works best with thick documents, where there are enough sheets to hold the glue.

- Side stabbing

The sheets are stapled together along the left hand edge. Very cheap, and pretty nasty too. For example, try getting the pages to stay open on their own!

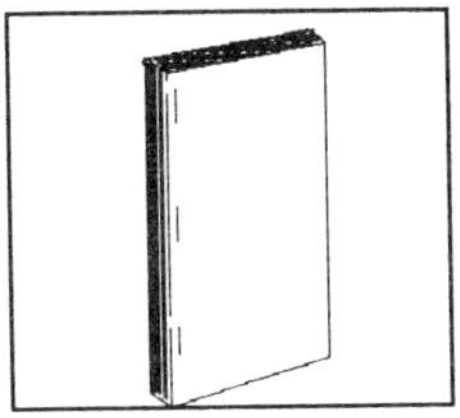

- Plastic grip binder

This holds the sheets along the left hand edge. Looks nice, is cheap and you can add or remove sheets easily. Unfortunately, though, the pages won't lie flat.

- Spiral binding

A coiled wire or plastic grip is fitted into holes made along the left hand edge. Cheap, and allows the pages to lie flat. However, they can take up a fair amount of room on a bookshelf. Also, impossible to print the name of the document along the spine.

- Canadian binding

This is spiral binding with an extra book cover added. It has the advantage of spiral binding of allowing the pages to be opened flat. At the same time it allows you to print the name of the document along the spine, making it easy to identify on the bookshelf. Unfortunately, the covers of Canadian bound books often tend to start looking tatty after a while.

- ❏ Saddle stitching

This is the method used for binding folded sheets. Pairs of pages are printed on the same sheets of paper, and sewn or stapled through the fold. Because each sheet contains 4 pages, documents bound by this method must contain a multiple of 4 pages.

Printing

There are several important aspects of printing:

- Printing resolution
- Postscript vs non-postscript printers
- Printer drivers and formatting
- Colour printing

Printing resolution

This has been covered in Chapter 1. There are, however, a couple of additional points that you may need to consider:

- The screen resolution and the print resolution are different. That means that you can't tell exactly what the document will look like until you print it - despite the fact that DTP programs are of the **WYSIWYG** (What You See Is What You Get) variety.
- The high resolution of laser printers enables the printouts to be used as draft copies the final copies being produced on a typesetter.
- Best results on a laser printer are obtained from laser printer or photocopier paper

Postscript vs non-postscript printers

Postscript is a page description language that describes what each part of the page is to look like. If your software allows you to save your work to disk in a format known as EPS - Encapsulated Postscript - then you don't necessarily need a postscript printer. You could send the disk containing your document to a printing bureau or commercial printer, who could then print out your document from the DOS prompt with a command such as:

C:>copy DOC_1.EPS PRN

which means:

"Send the document called DOC_1.EPS to the printer."

Your document will then be printed out exactly as it looked on your screen.

Notice that no mention has been made of the commercial printer having to have the software you used. Postscript is a universal language: an EPS file produced by one program is exactly the same as that produced by any other program.

As a consequence of this, you and your commercial printer do not need to have the same software as far as the printing of the document is concerned. You could be using a "bargain basement" shareware program costing £10, and they could be using a top package costing £700. As long as your program can save files in EPS format, it won't matter.

Another consequence is that draft copies produced on a Postscript laser printer will give you a precise idea of what the final (typeset) document will look like - that is, if you're **having** the document printed on a typesetter.

Postscript printers require more RAM and, partly because of this, tend to be more expensive. Moreover, some programs, such as Calamus on the Atari ST, do not support Postscript anyway.

However, having used both Postscript and non-Postscript printers, I have found the former to be much faster. For example, a page from this book takes on average 5 minutes to print on a non-Postscript printer and about 25 seconds on a Postscript one. Now, if you are producing a 20 page newsletter, that probably doesn't matter too much. However, attempting to produce a 200 page book at the rate of 12 pages an hour is, frankly, ridiculous. Even if you don't mind the printer working continuously overnight , or you are one of those people who can finish their work three weeks before the deadline, such slow printing speeds effectively rule out substantial last-minute revisions.

Recently, relatively inexpensive but powerful laser printers using non-Postscript Page Description Languages have been developed. Laser printers which use them are, by and large, cheaper than their Postscript relatives. However, it is too early to say whether these or other developments - such as Adobe Type Manager - are good enough to render Postscript printers almost completely unnecessary.

Printer drivers and formatting

A printer driver is software that drives the printer. What it does, in effect, is to say to the DTP program:

"This document is going to be printed on a Bloggs EX24 24 pin printer. Therefore, to make the printer understand that this word is to be printed in bold type, you will have to give this style the following code...", and so on. As you might expect, different printers understand different codes, and so require different printer drivers.

One of the consequences of this when using some DTP programs is that if you format a document with one printer driver loaded, and then print it out using a different printer driver, some of the formatting can go awry. For example, you may discover a few widows and orphans that were not there before.

You may wonder when you are likely to print out a document using a different printer driver to the one you had originally set up.

Suppose you were producing a document that was to be printed out on a laser printer which you do not have. You would probably obtain draft copies as you went along, using a dot matrix printer perhaps. When satisfied with the document, you would then have the disk delivered to the person responsible for the printing.

A good idea is to insert an extra stage in the process. After your final proof-reading and before delivering the disk, set up the program with the printer driver for the printer to be used in the final printing. Then examine the document on-screen in order to ensure that the formatting is still all right.

Colour printing

Colour printing is becoming less and less expensive, and there are a number of options open to you. However, you need to be clear on why you want a colour printer. If it is to produce draft copy of a full colour publication which will be produced by a commercial printer, you will need a printer capable of reproducing exactly the colours used in commercial printing. These printers are expensive.

If your requirements are not quite as stringent as this, colour printing starts to look more reasonable.

Colour printing can be achieved by the following means:

- Colour dot matrix printers
- Inkjet printers
- Thermal transfer printers
- Dye-sublimation printers
- Laser printers

Colour dot matrix printers

These are very reasonably priced, and produce passable results. Unfortunately, as the ribbon gets worn the colours start to look duller and duller.

Inkjet printers

These produce very vibrant colours but can be costly to run. Specialised inkjet printers are available which faithfully reproduce Pantone colours.(See page 10.7)

Thermal transfer printers

These are useful for producing overhead projector transparencies and are inexpensive to run. On the minus side, they can be rather slow because each page is printed three or four times - once for each colour.

Dye-sublimation printers

These are capable of producing printouts which could easily be mistaken for photographs. As you might expect, though, they are expensive to buy and expensive to run.

Laser printers

These offer both speed and quality - at a price. However, prices are coming down. A few years ago it would have been inconceivable that virtually anyone could have a (monochrome) laser printer sitting on their desk at home. But that is now almost a realty. The same thing is set to happen with colour laser printers.

Moreover, the increasing tendency for them to have Postscript compatibility makes them more and more feasible an option for meeting all of ones desktop publishing needs.

Colour printing bureaux

If you need colour printing only occasionally, it makes sense to use a bureau than to buy an expensive printer. Bureaux will undertake printing, transparency making and 35mm slide production from your disks.

Colour camera-ready copy

Producing colour camera-ready copy - ie printouts that a commercial printer can use as a basis for the final printing - is a skilled and complex job. In fact, it is beyond the scope of this book to delve into great technical detail about it.

Printing in colour yourself might be useful to give you an idea of what the final document will look like. However, there's more to producing camera-ready artwork than simply printing a coloured copy.

In fact, the printer will require several copies of your work:

either

- One for each colour - the **spot** colour method

or

- Just four, corresponding to cyan, yellow, magenta and black - the **process** colour method

You will therefore need to buy DTP software that supports one or both of these. The software should also be capable of printing registration marks on the paper. These enable the printer to align all the colour sheets for each page accurately.

It is also useful to be able to specify a Pantone colour - either in the software itself or not. All printers use inks corresponding to the **Pantone Matching System**. Select the colour you want from a book of Pantone colours. Then see your printer and specify the colours you want in terms of the Pantone system. This will ensure that you get **exactly** what you want.

Page positioning

If your document is going to consist of pages formed by folding the paper then you need to be aware of where the pages will be positioned in the document.

Suppose you are producing a 4 page document. The pages are to be A5 in size, formed by folding two A4 sheets in half. This is how the pages will be positioned:

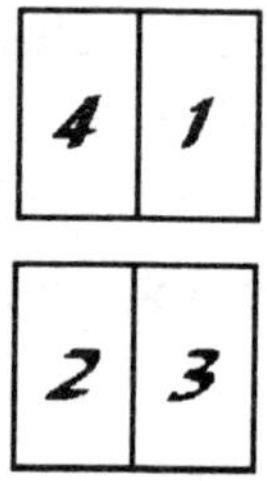

This shows you that the last page - page 4 - will be printed on the left hand side of the same sheet as the first page - page 1. Pages 2 and 3 appear next to each other in the correct order.

For an 8 page document, the positioning seems more complex, but follows the same logic. However, a commercial printer will advise you on the best way of organising your document, and will actually do it for you at the printing stage.

Collating

Some printers have a collating option which can come into play when you want more than one copy of a document. This prints the pages in their correct order. The trouble is, every time the printer has printed one page, it loses the information when it starts on the next. Therefore if it has taken 5 minutes to pass the information about each page from the computer to the printer, you will have to wait another 5 minutes when it comes to doing that page again.

A quicker option is to ask for multiple copies **without** collation, and then collate them yourself afterwards, or put them through a collating machine.

Project 1: A simple letterhead

In this project you will create a letterhead to use as a template for future correspondence. It is assumed that you have set the paper length etc already.

What you will need

- Your address!

Skills covered

- Drawing a frame
- Typing directly into the frame or page
- Creating a special style for the address
- Saving the letter as a template

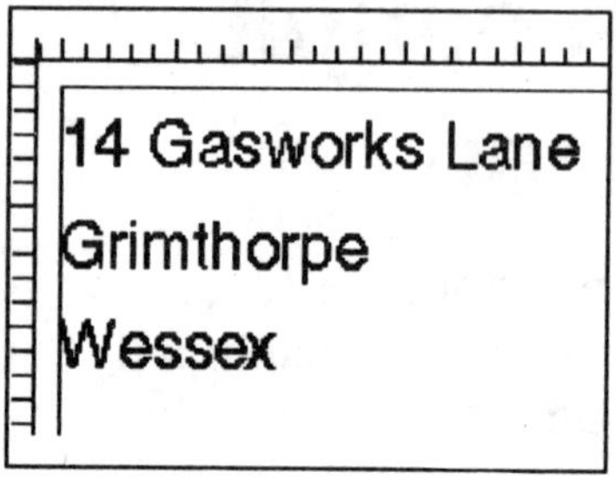

First, type your address onto the page or frame.

Then change the style associated with that text...*

* If this facility exists!

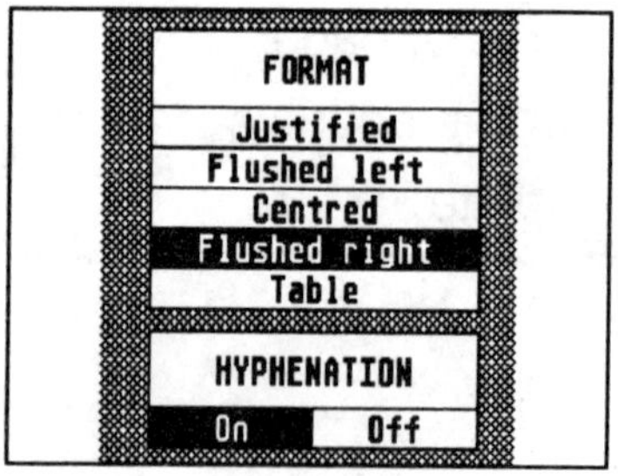

...so that the text is aligned ie lined up, on the right hand edge.

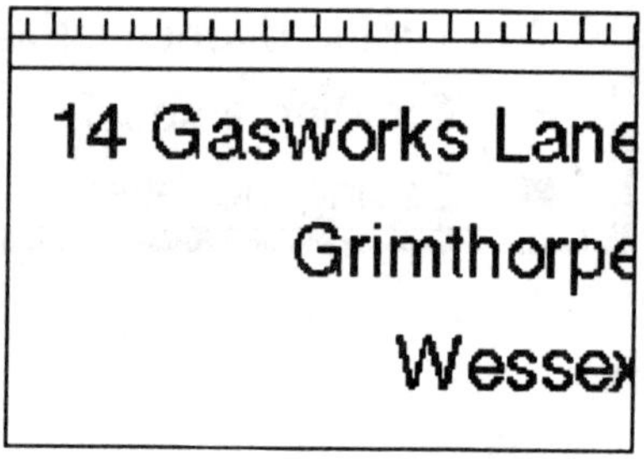

This is the result.

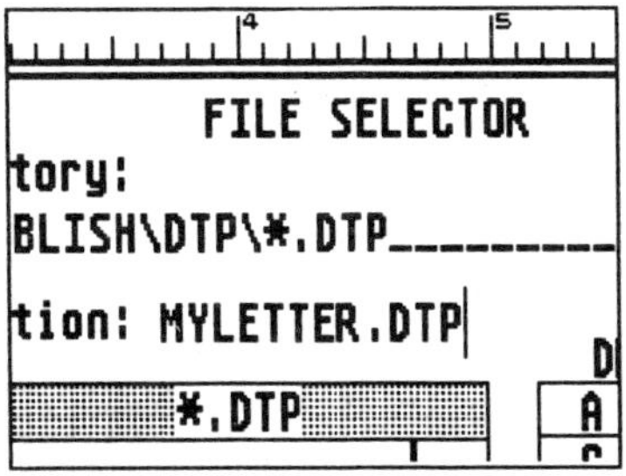

Save the (almost) blank page to use as a template in future...

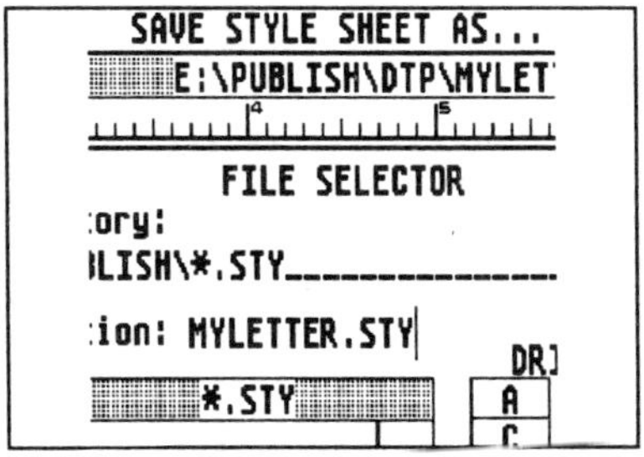

...or save the layout or style sheet for use in other documents.

Project 2: A letter

In this project you will use the simple letterhead created in Project 1 as a basis for formatting a letter.

What you will need

- The letterhead created and saved in Project 1
- Word processed text - just a few paragraphs will do

Skills covered

- Opening a document
- Importing text

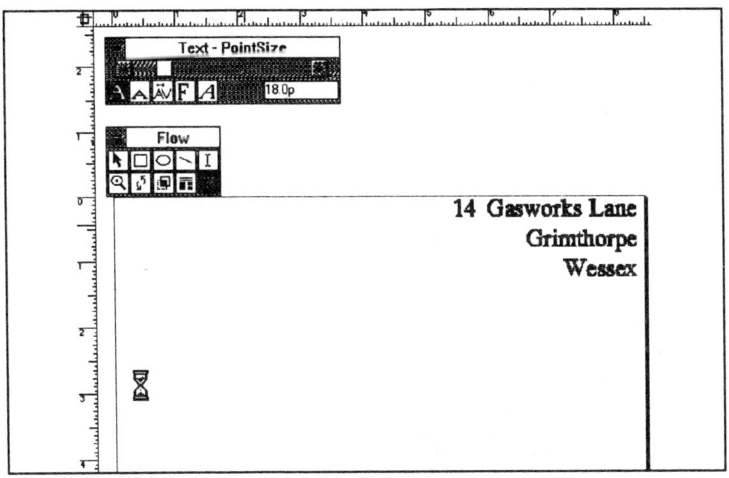

First, load the letterhead from Project 1

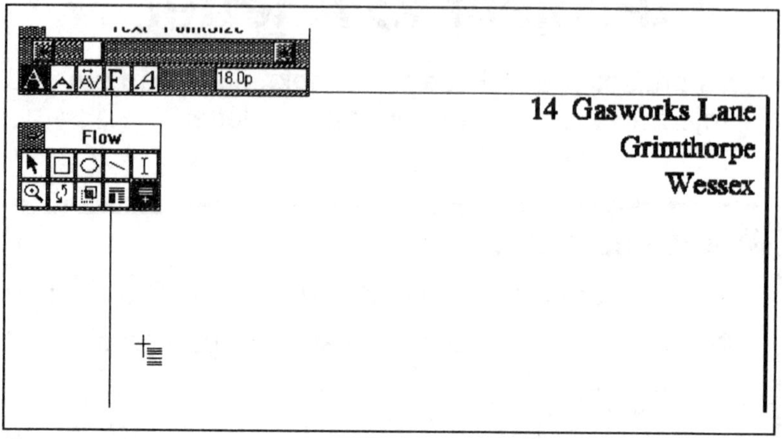

Next, import the text. In this example, it will appear at the mouse pointer.

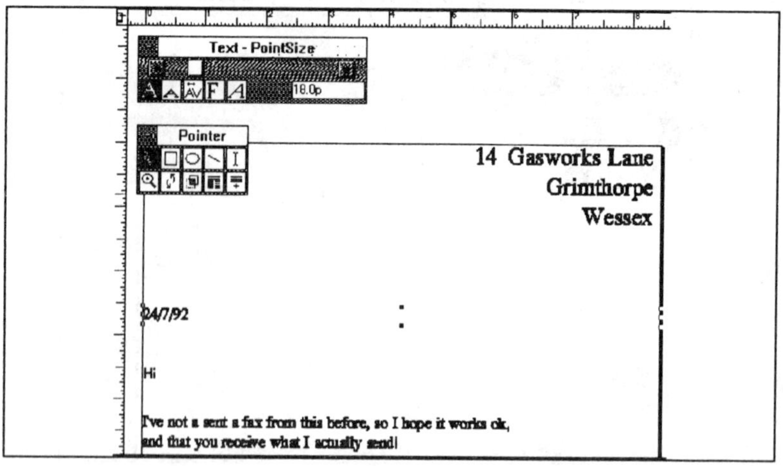

The text has been imported, and put in the correct place.

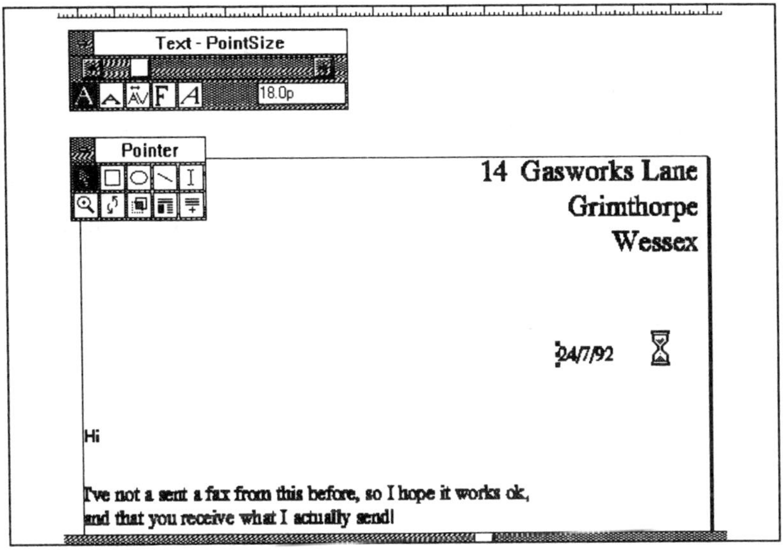

The date is moved over to the right by using a right-justified paragraph style.

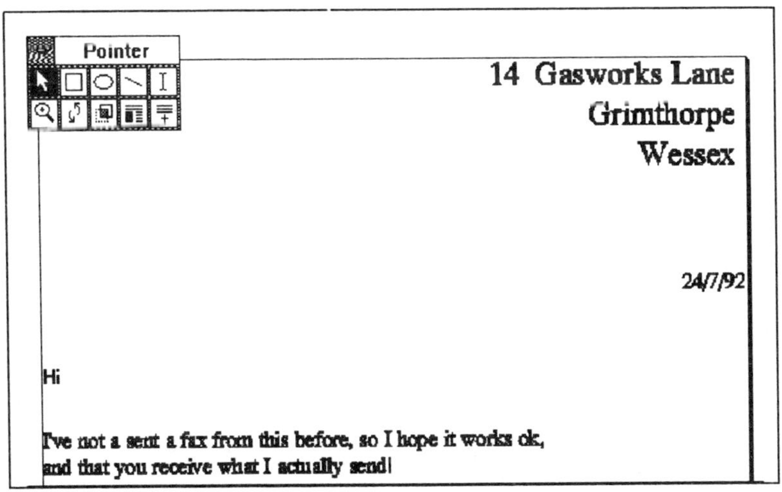

Voila! Save this by a different name, and the original letterhead will remain intact. See overleaf if you use a frame-based program.

If you use a frame-based program you can save yourself a bit of time and trouble over the long run by using a very simple trick:

Put the address in its own, small, frame. Then create another frame for the body of the letter.

By doing this, you will never have to mess about trying to put the cursor in the right place before importing the letter text. All you'll need to do is go into text mode and then click in the main frame.

Project 3: Letterhead with logo

Rather than have just an ordinary letterhead, you may prefer to have one which incorporates a picture.

In the example used here, the graphic consists of a "handwritten" effect which was created in a painting package. However, the principles involved are exactly the same as if a "proper" drawing was used.

What you will need

- A previously-created graphic to use as a logo

Skills covered

- Importing a graphic
- Drawing and resizing frames

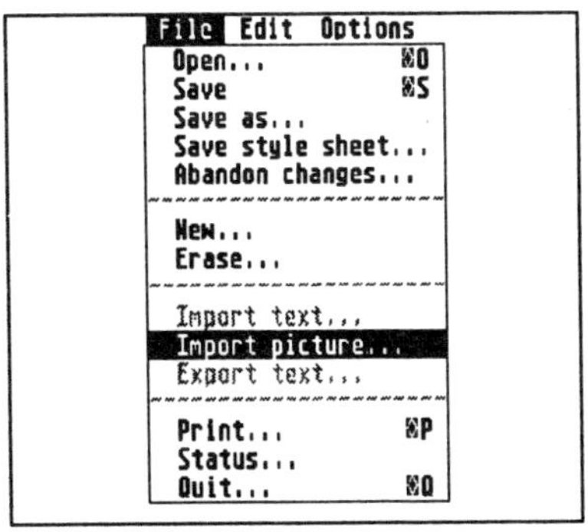

First, import the graphic...

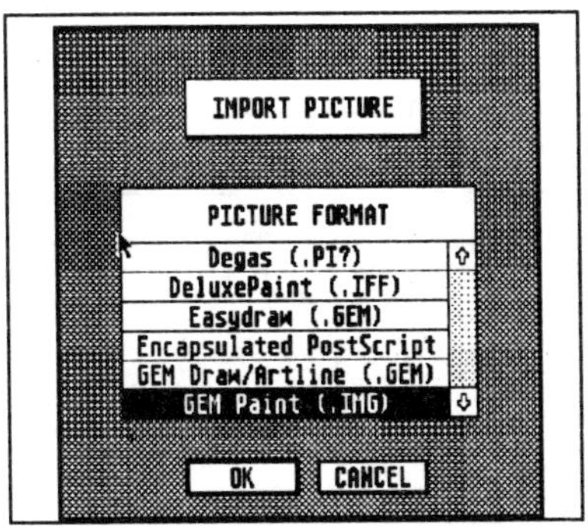

...you may need to specify the type.

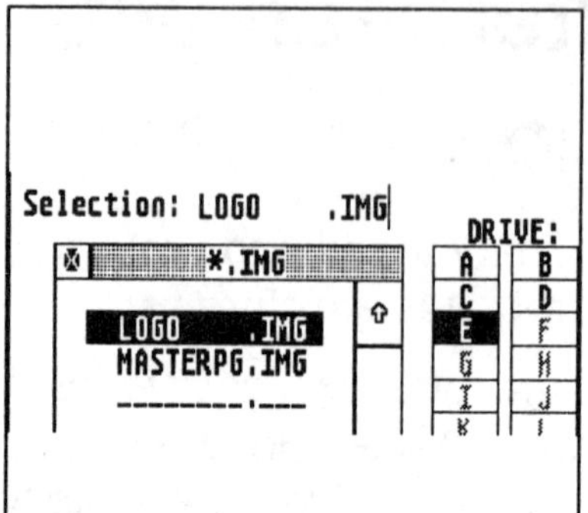

Select the graphic you want to use.

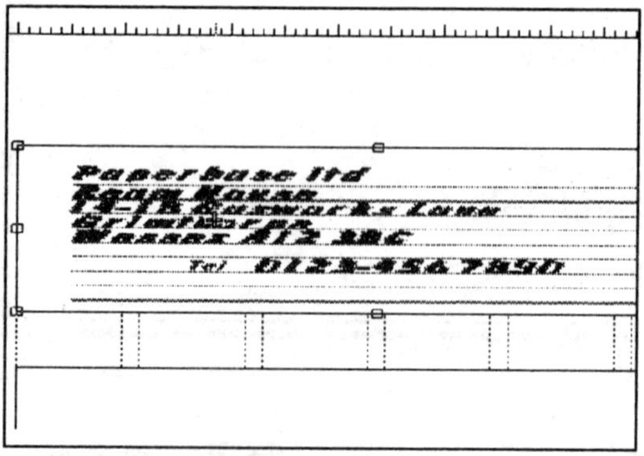

In this example, the picture has been imported into a frame. As you can see, it's somewhat distorted...

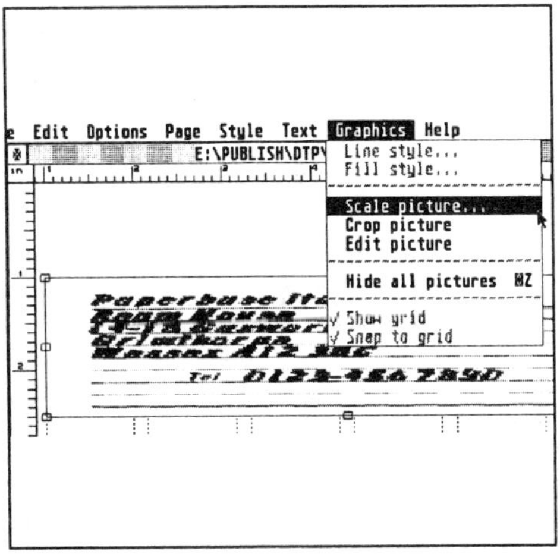

...and so needs rescaling.

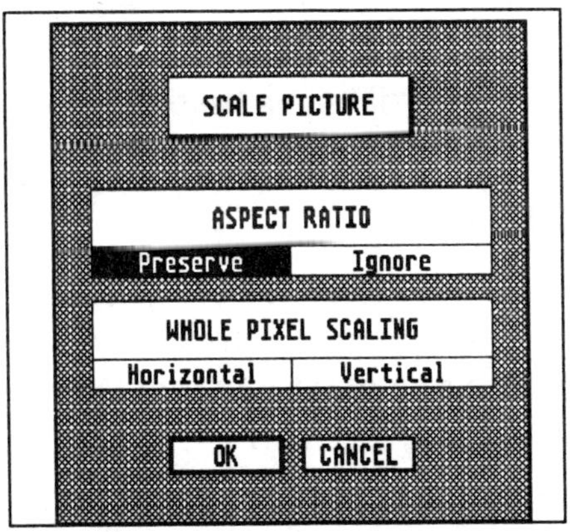

The **aspect ratio** is the relationship between the vertical and the horizontal aspects of the graphic. In this example, the aspect ratio was lost initially. By preserving it, the picture will appear less distorted.

In this particular DTP program (Timeworks Publisher 2), you can fine tune the aspect ratio even further by the use of whole pixel scaling. This helps to avoid moiré patterns appearing in the printed graphic.

As you can see, the graphic is no longer distorted.

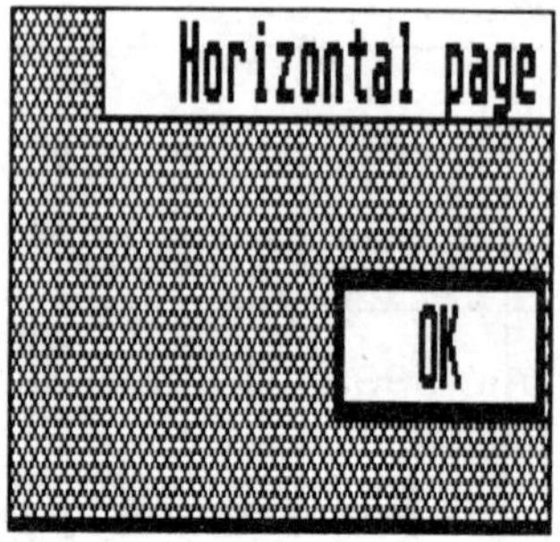

An example of a moiré pattern.

Different programs have different ways of enabling you to rescale graphics while maintaining their correct proportions, such as:

- Selecting a menu entry for scaling or rescaling, in which you specify the aspect ratios manually
- Changing the size of the picture by resizing it while the Alt, Shift or Control key is held down
- Clicking on an icon
- Using a keyboard shortcut

Once you've positioned the logo exactly where you want it, save the document as a template. In this way, you can always use it as a basis for all of your letters.

Project 4: A simple poster

A poster is a notice that is intended to be read by passers-by. It therefore has to be quite eye-catching. It has to make enough of an impact to make the person who sees it want to stop and read more.

Let's take a fairly ordinary example, that of a notice for a concert in the local village hall.

What you will need

- Nothing!

Skills covered

- Drawing frames
- Formatting text
- Using different fonts

The Village Green
presents

The Blues People
in concert

Friday 18th September 1992

Doors Open 7.30

Tickets £5 on the door

Refreshments available

Type in the text directly on to the page, or into the program's text editor - if there is one. (There is not enough text to justify using a word processor). As you can see, the appearance of the poster leaves something to be desired!

In order to make the poster more attractive, you can highlight the top line (usually by pressing and holding down the left mouse button and dragging the mouse pointer over the text).

Next, select another font. Note that an alternative method in some programs is to make the heading a different paragraph style.

The font has been changed from serif to sans serif, and the type enlarged. It has also been centred, by highlighting it and clicking on the centering icon shown above right.

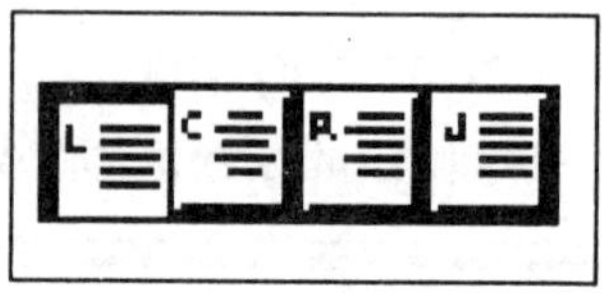

Icons like these make formatting the text a fairly easy task.

Using these techniques, and by adding a little more line space between "in concert" and "Friday...", the poster opposite has been produced.

The final result

Project 5: A poster with graphics

They say a picture speaks a thousand words, and this is especially true of posters. An appropriate and well-placed picture can grab the passer-by's attention and make them want to find out what it's all about.

In this project we take the poster produced in Project 4 and embellish it with a picture.

What you will need

- The poster you produced in Project 4
- A previously created picture of a harmonica

Skills covered

- Opening a document
- Importing graphics
- Cropping pictures
- Resizing pictuers

This is the poster we created last time...

...and this is how it will look when it's been amended.

First, draw a frame for the picture. Note that in some DTP programs you can skip this step.

Next, import the picture. This is usually an option in the File menu.

There are unwanted areas here, so the cropping function is selected...

The dotted lines indicate which parts of the picture will be left once you've finished cropping it.

This looks much better now. However, look how the graphic has pushed the text out of the way. Unfortunately, it's done so by splitting the words up in an unacceptable manner.

Hold the left mouse button down and drag the picture over to the right.

And here we are! Because this is a screen shot, and one which has been greatly enlarged, the lettering looks jagged. If your DTP program uses vector or outline fonts, rather than bitmapped fonts, this won't happen.

Project 6: Poster with a border

Sometimes you can enhance the appearance of a poster by adding a border to it. This is a fairly straightforward procedure which involves drawing a frame around the perimeter of the poster and then making choices about such things as the thickness of the border and whether it is plain or patterned.

What you will need

- The poster you created in Project 5

Skills covered

- Opening a document
- Drawing a border
- Choosing/changing the border attributes

First, open the document which you created in Project 5 - the poster advertising a concert. It is shown here with its frame selected, as shown by the little black squares (handles) around the edge.

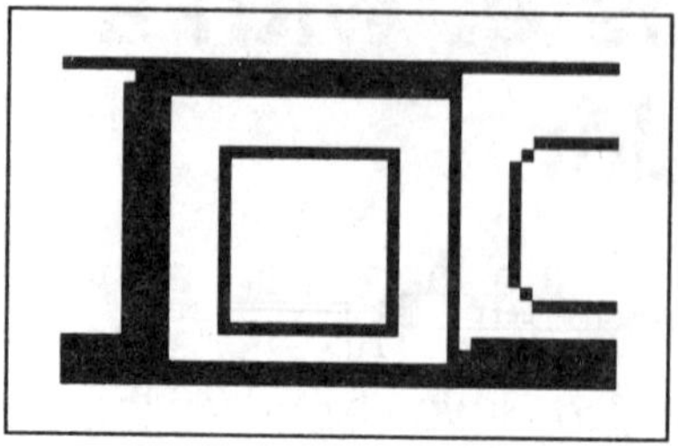

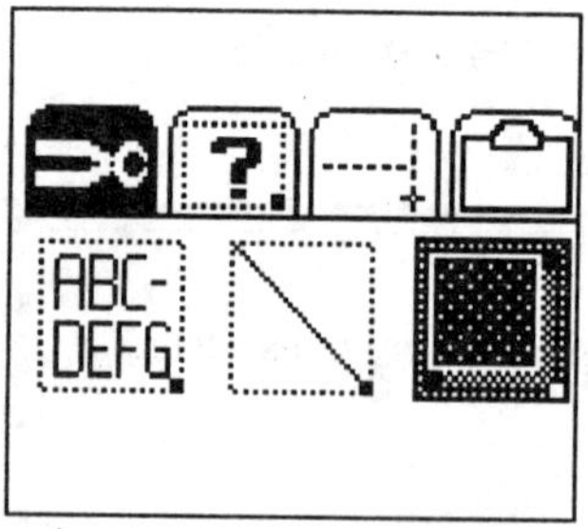

The next step is to select the border drawing tool. This is normally indicated as an icon, as shown in the three examples here (shown highlighted). Some programs, like Timeworks Publisher 2, require you to draw an ordinary frame and then give it a border.

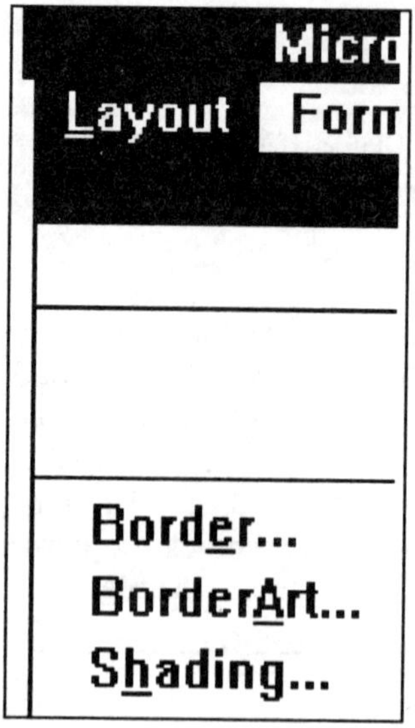

Once you've drawn the border or frame you need to set its attributes. This may be done either through a menu system or by clicking on icons. Both methods are shown here and on the facing page.

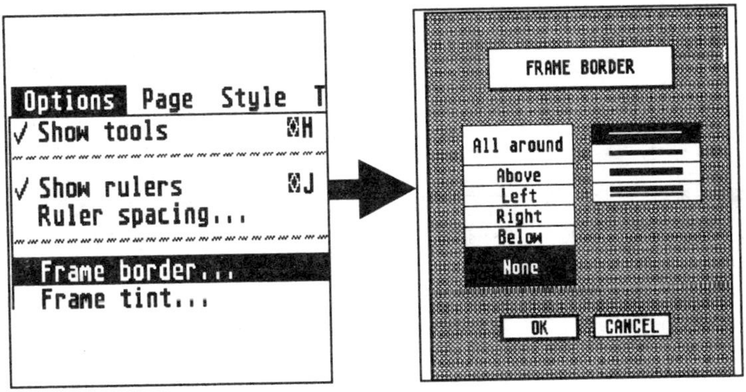

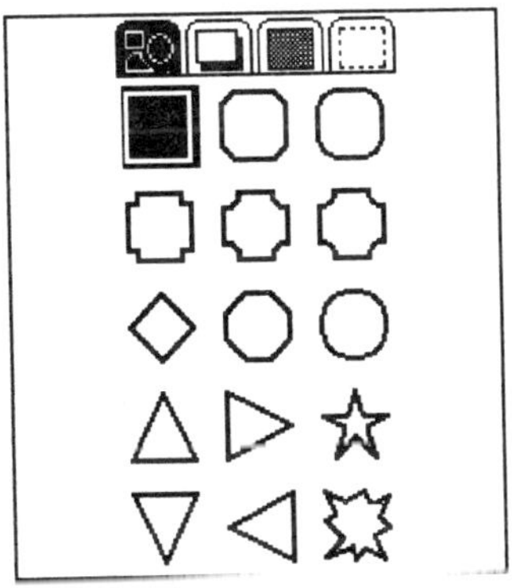

These screen shots and the one on the previous page illustrate the various means by which you can configure some of the attributes of the frame border.

As well as selecting the shape of the border and, in some programs, whether it is visible all the way round or on one or more sides of the frame, you can often choose the thickness of the lines and even the pattern of the border. Examples are shown over the page.

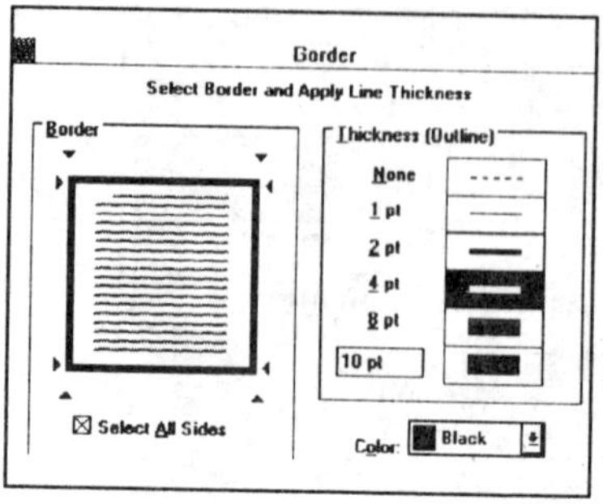

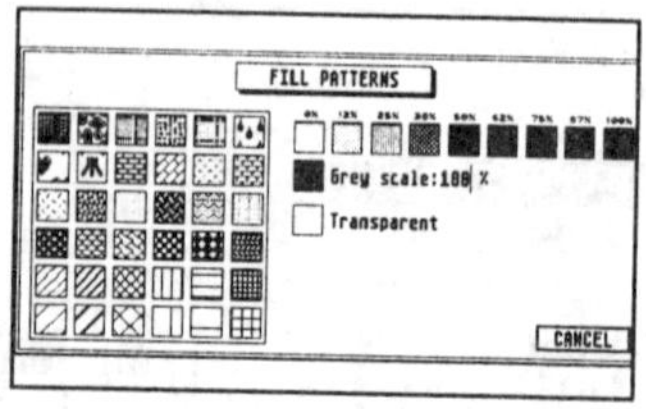

Examples of selection of border thickness (left) and border pattern (above).

Returning to the task in hand, the picture on the left shows what the frame border looks like after it has been made thicker. The steps involved were: select the frame or draw the border and select that, and then change its attributes.

Rather than simply making the border of the poster thicker, you could give it a pattern of some kind. The page opposite shows two examples of this - one from Calamus, the other from Microsoft Publisher.

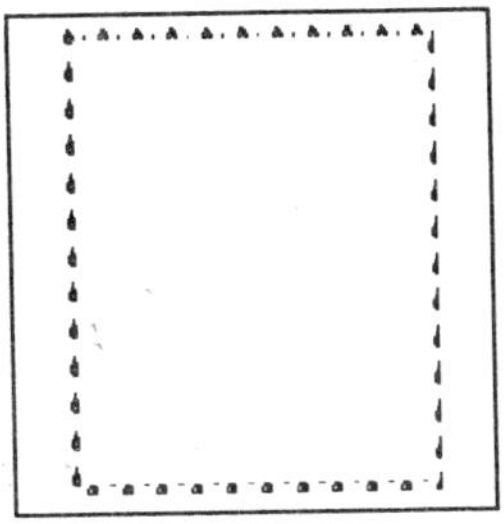

This shows a patterned border created in Calamus. The following effect was achieved with Microsoft Publisher.

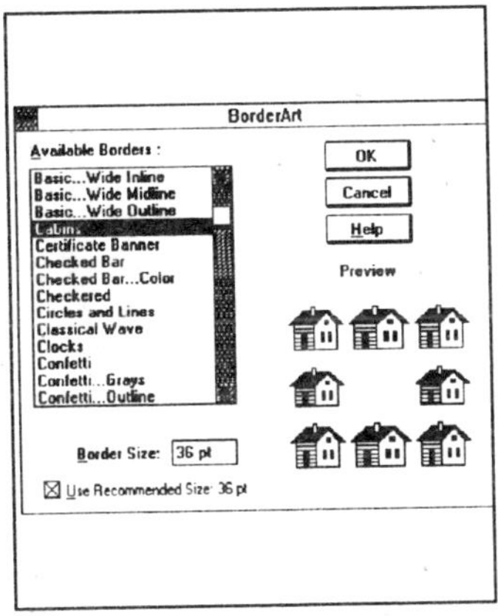

In some DTP programs you can have a border made up from clip art. This can make for a very interesting effect. Instead of setting the border thickness, you choose the clip art to be used, and the program does the rest.

In this particular example, the border art was too large, and so it affected the layout (above). The border could have been made thinner, but in this case it was decided to resize the picture of the harmonica instead (left).

Suppose you'd like to create the effect shown on the previous page, but you don't have a program with a border art facility?

All is not lost! The next project shows you how you can achieve your ambition.

Project 7: Creating a border

In Project 6 you produced a poster with a border which consisted of clip art. That was easy because the DTP program used to illustrate the project contained a border art facility.

What if your program lacks this facility? No problem! You can still create the same effect; it just takes a little bit longer, that's all.

For the sake of clarity, the illustrations given here depict the border only, not the poster itself.

What you will need

- A previously-created picture

Skills covered

- Importing a picture
- Resizing a picture
- Copying a frame
- Selecting several frames
- Copying several frames
- Moving frames

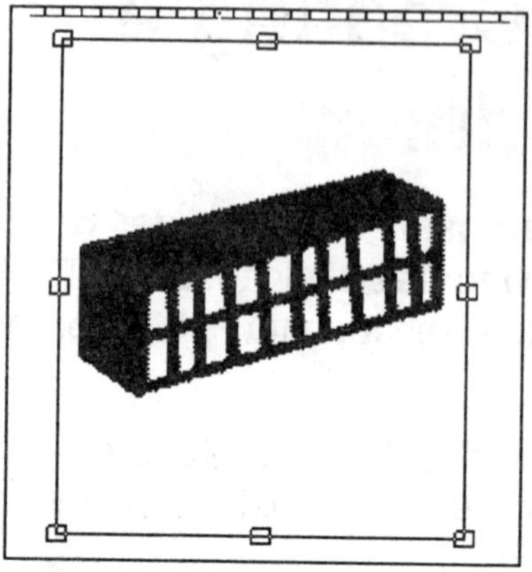

First, draw an appropriate picture in a painting program, or use clip art. Note that a harmonica is being used, since this is more appropriate for a blues concert poster than is a cabin!

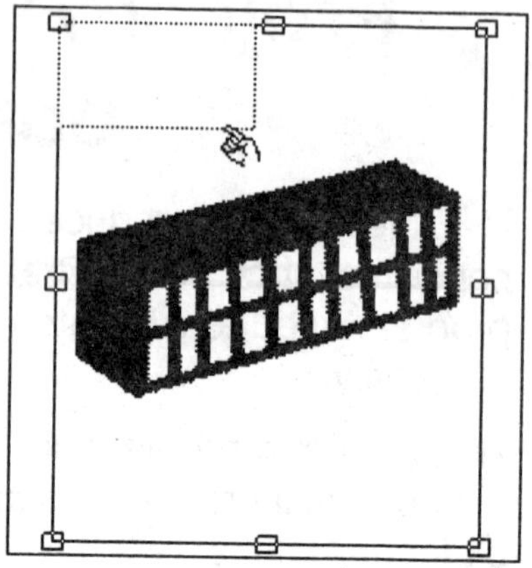

Next, resize the frame until it is small enough to form part of a border...

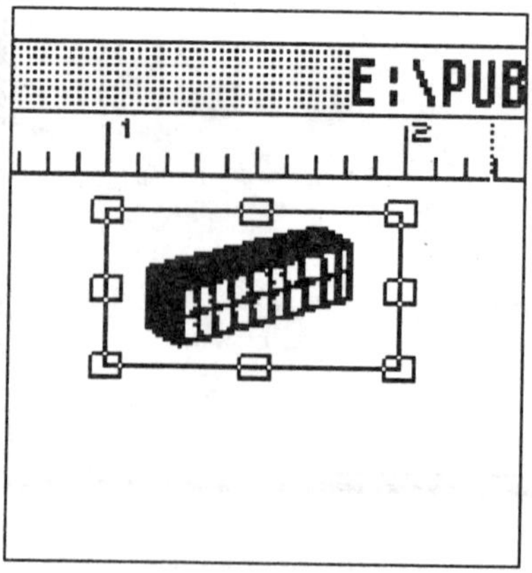

...This is probably about the right size.

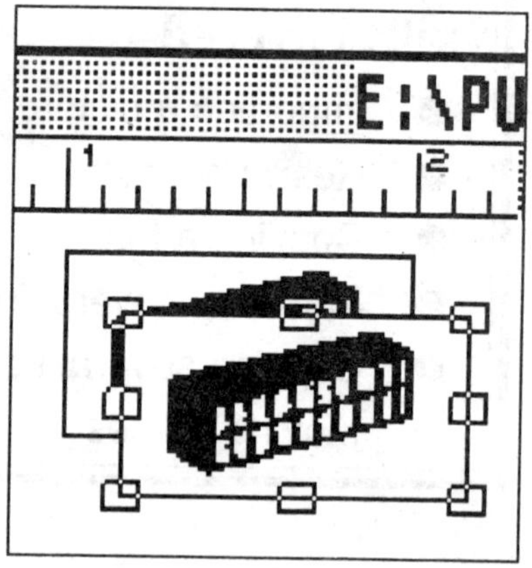

Now copy the frame and paste it. There are now two identical frames.

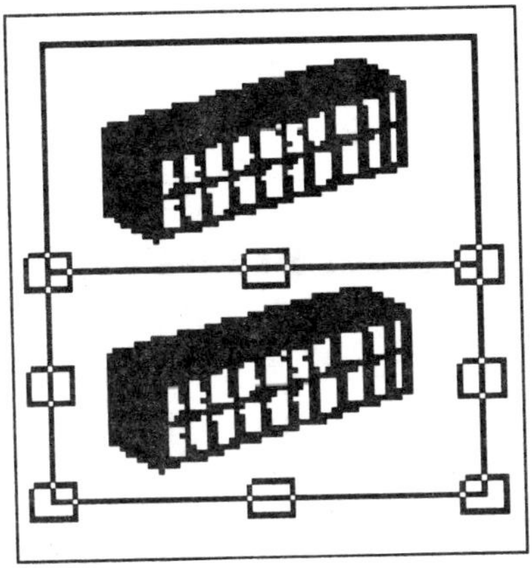

Align the frames one on top of the other. If you have a snap-to-guides option use it, because it will help you align the frames exactly, and get the spacing right.

When you've done this with several frames, use the **Select all** function to select all of them together - or select several by doing it "manually".

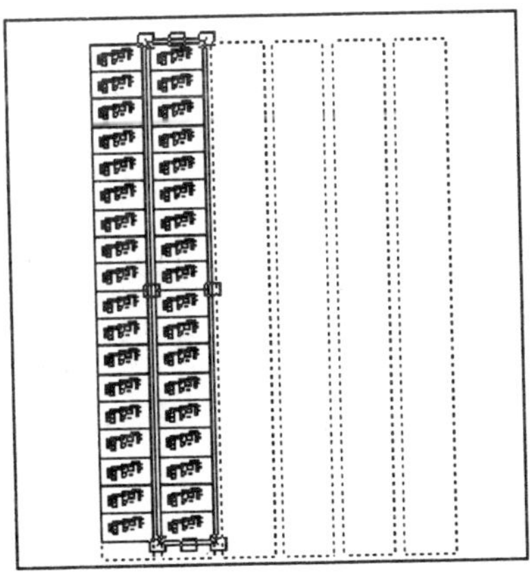

Then copy them all in one go. Move the copied frames to the correct position - all at once.

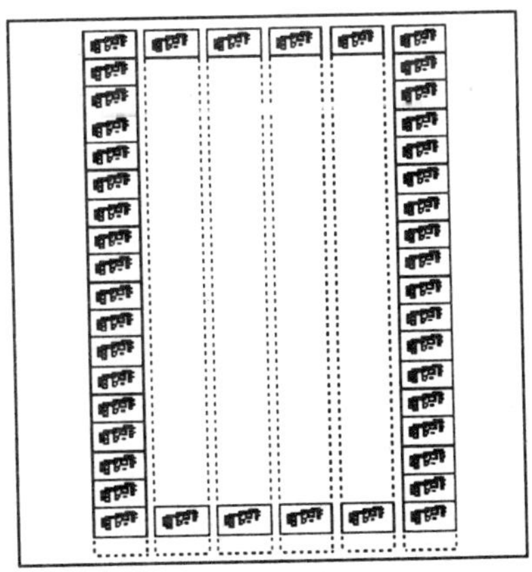

Continue like this in order to get through the task much more quickly.

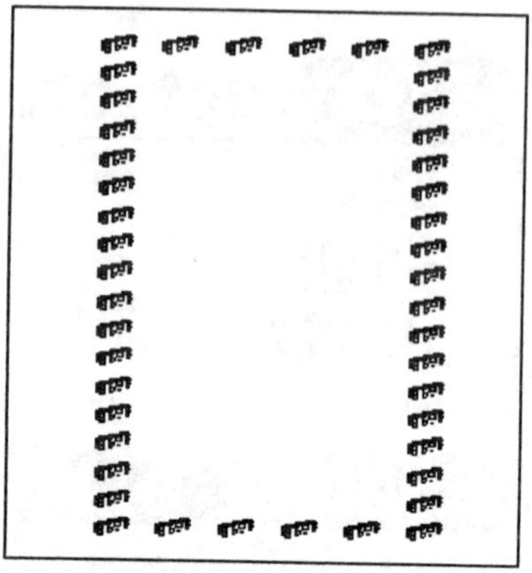

And here is the result.

All of the skills covered in the first seven projects will be applied in the next few projects. These are concerned with business stationery.

Project 8: Creating memos

In this and the three projects following the theme is business stationery. Taken overall, the three projects indicate how a house style can be created over different types of business stationery - in particular, memos, compliments slips, business cards and invoices.

You can use your imagination to extend the concept to, say, letterheads and price lists.

What you will need

- A graphic to use as a logo

Skills covered

- Importing graphics
- Copying and pasting frames
- Copying and pasting lines
- Moving frames

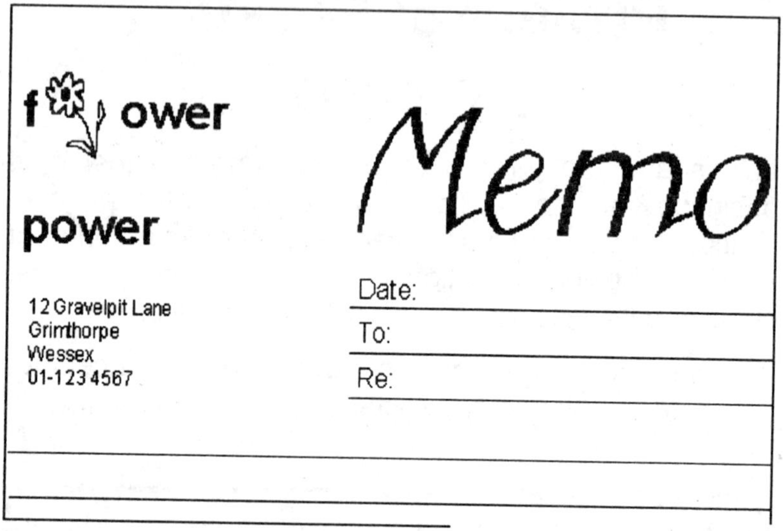

This is how the finished product will look.

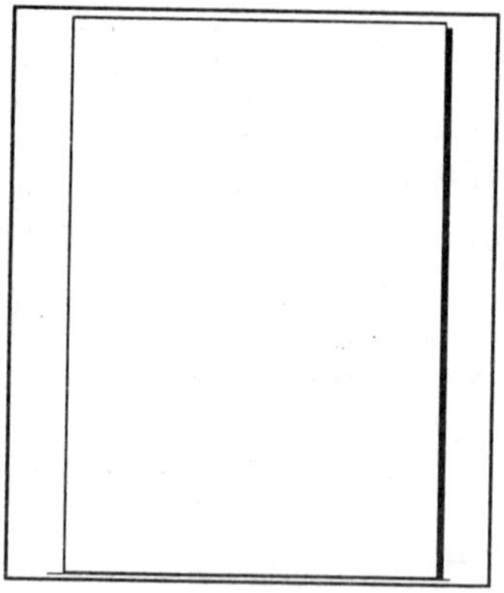

First, start with an empty frame.

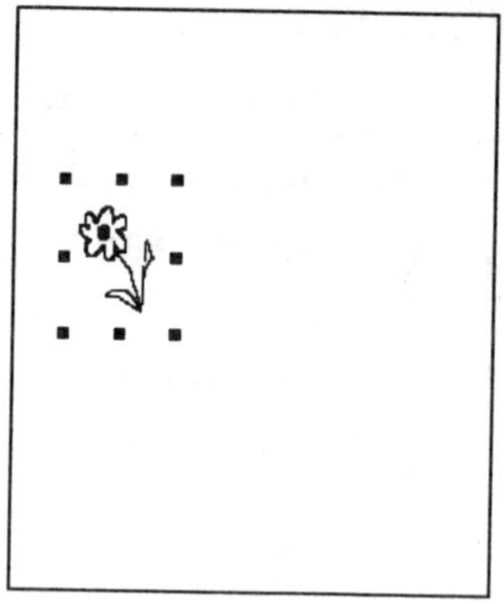

Then import a picture that you've created beforehand.

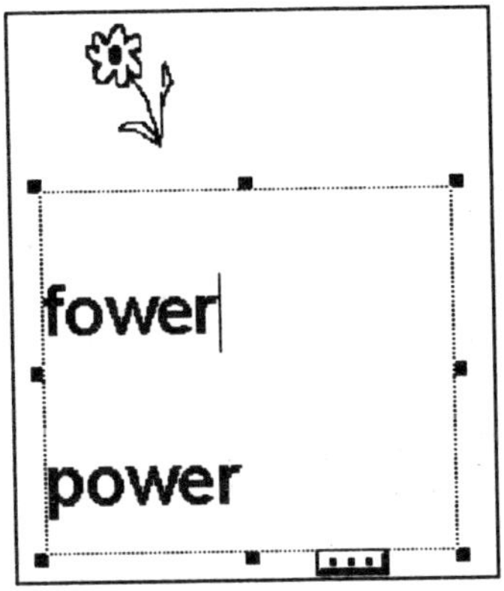

Next, draw a text frame and type the words "fower power".

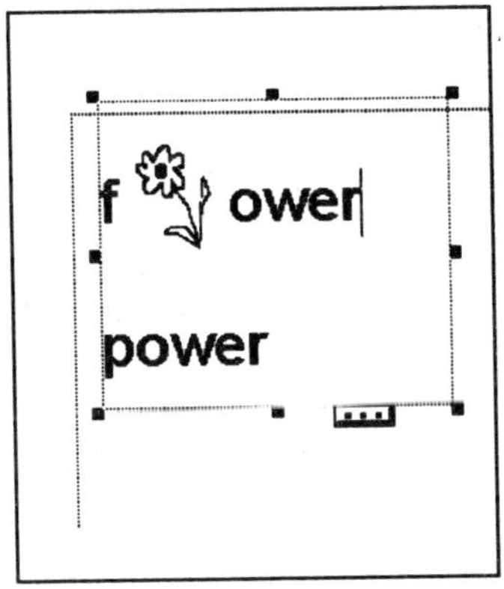

Now move the text frame up until it covers the picture of the flower. The flower should cause the word "fower" to flow around it. You may have to experiment with the "bring to front/back options" though.

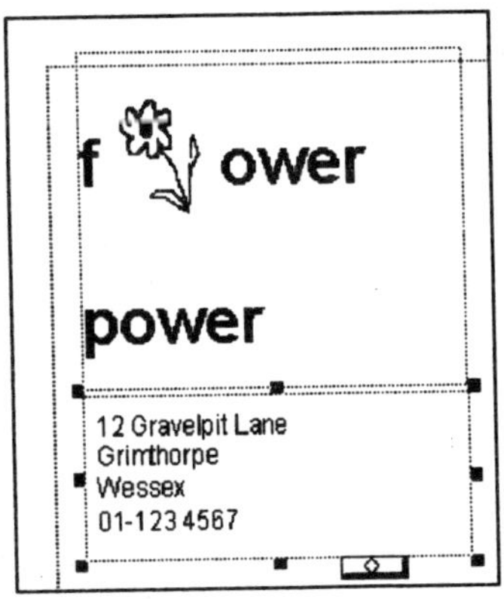

Now, in another text frame, type the address etc.

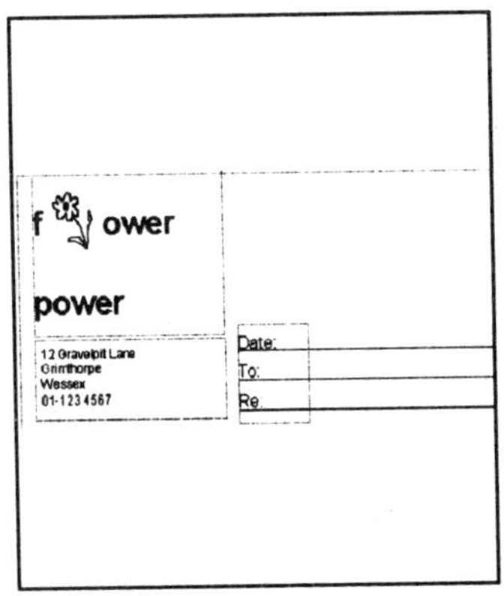

In yet another text frame type "Date:","To:" and "Re:" Then, using the line drawing facility, add a few lines.

The final stage is to insert the word "Memo". In the example shown here, Word Art, which comes built-in to Microsoft Publisher, has been used. A similar product is Type Plus, by Serif. Alternatively, a separate graphics program could have been used, and the result **imported** into the document.

You can use certain elements of this document again, in different but related documents. In the next project, an invoice is created using the same logo and address style.

If you are using a Windows program, doing this is easy: you just select the frames you want to use again, copy them, open a new document, and paste them.

If you are not using a Windows program you may need to be more resourceful. You may, for example, be able to save just one page of this document, load it up as a separate document, and cut out the bits you don't need. Or perhaps you could **export** the parts you need, and import them into a new document. Use your imagination!

Project 9: Creating invoices

Continuing the theme of business stationery, this project looks at the creation of invoices. It also looks at the creation of a house style by using certain elements from the memo created in Project 8. To make life a little easier for yourself in that respect, take a look at the suggestions made at the end of that project, on page 18.4

What you will need

- The logo and address panel from Project 8

Skills covered

- Importing graphics
- Pasting frames from another document
- Cutting and pasting frames within a document
- Creating and positioning lines
- Using tabs
- Positioning text

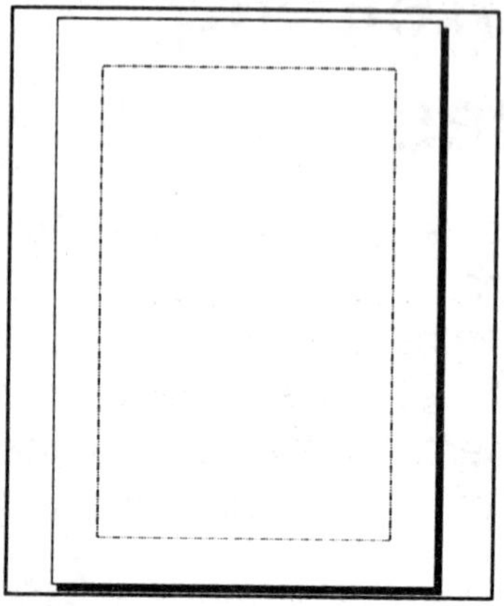

First, start with a blank page as usual.

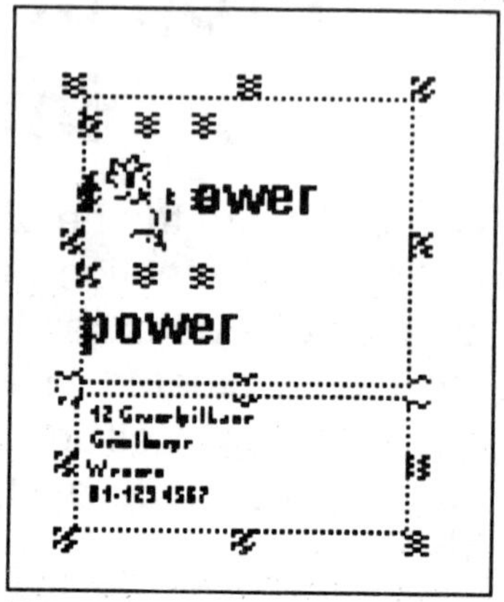

Next, import or paste in the logo and the address panel.

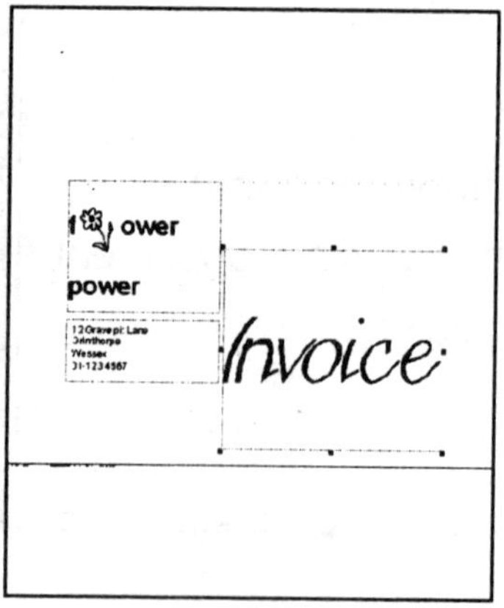

Then create the title "Invoice" in the same way as you created the title "Memo" in the previous project.

Now draw a box for the column titles. Take a copy of this box, but don't paste it just yet.

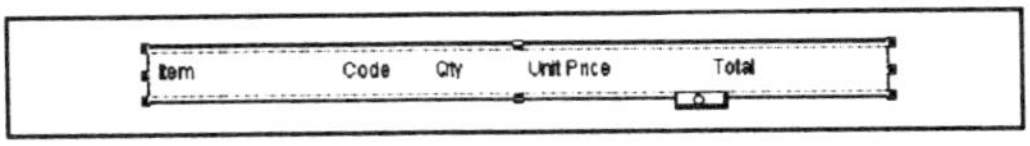

In this box, draw a text frame (if necessary), and type the words "Item", "Code", "Qty", "Unit Price" and "Total". Separate them by tabs, not spaces, and then set the tabs so that the text appears as shown here.

Depending on the program you are using, you will either have to set the tabs by clicking on the ruler, clicking on an icon, selecting an item from a format or layout menu, or configure a special paragraph style.

Happy hunting!

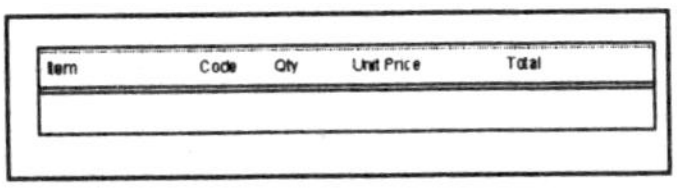

Now you can paste the box you copied earlier, and position it under and next to the first one. The snap-to-grid option is useful here, since it will help you align the two frames exactly. If you can specify that the border of the second frame is invisible on top, then double thickness lines where the two boxes touch will be avoided.

After adding a few more boxes like that (simply by continuing to paste them), the document is starting to take shape.

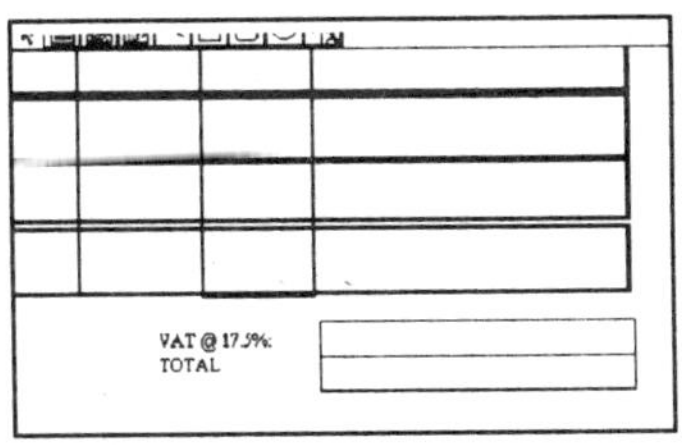

Then add the vertical lines - either by drawing boxes or using the line drawing tool - and add the VAT and TOTAL boxes and labels. If you are using a frame-based package, the labels will be easier to position if you draw a text frame especially for them.

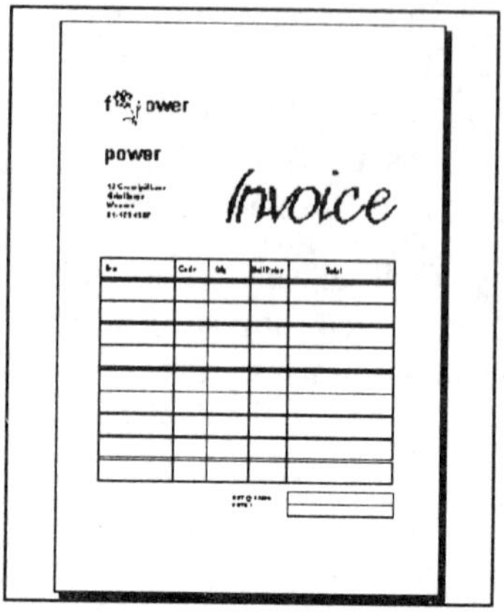

This is how the document looks at the moment.

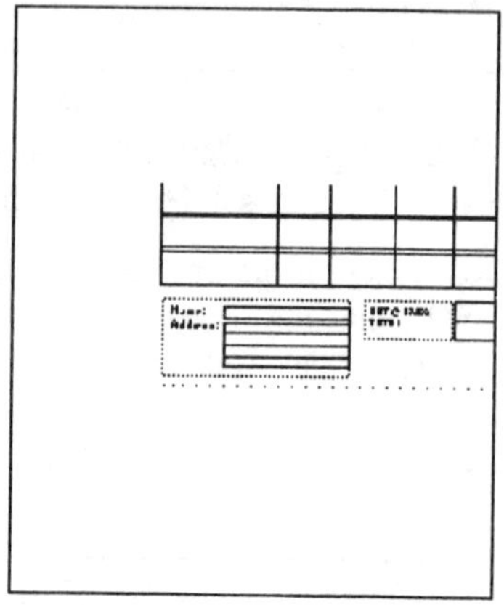

Now draw boxes and labels for the customer's name & address.

And here is the finished product. The memo document has been added for comparison. Notice the existence of a house style?

Project 10: Creating a compliments slip

Once again, we look at how to produce an item of business stationery. By now, you should be getting the hang of how to do it! Look at the previous two projects for extra guidance if you need to.

What you will need

- The logo and address panel from Project 8

Skills covered

- Importing graphics
- Pasting frames from another document
- Using measurements

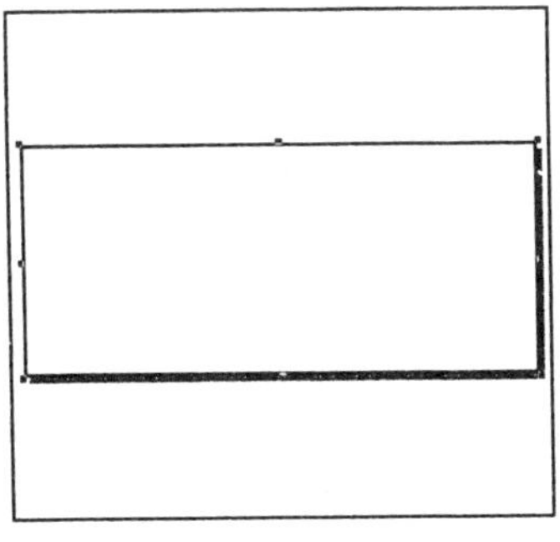

Start with a blank page and draw a frame. Make the frame the exact size you want by using one of the methods given in Chapter 6. Compliments slips come in all shapes and sizes; 6" by 3" or similar is often used.

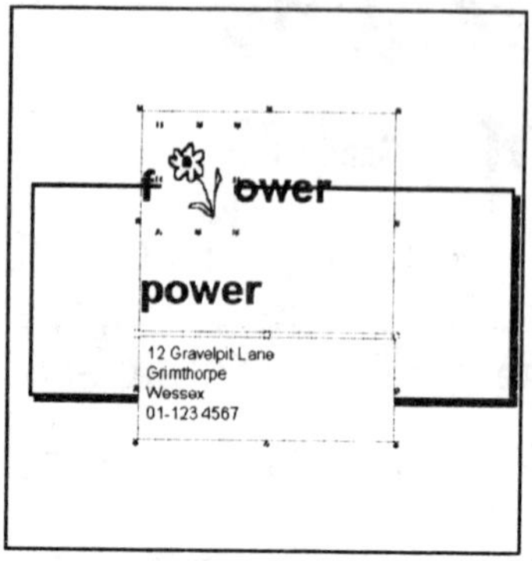

Next, import or paste in the logo and address panel. Move the address panel out of the way...

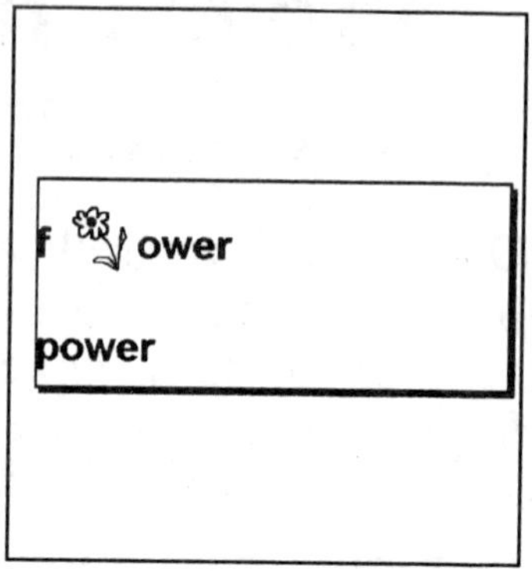

...and place the logo in position on the left hand side of the compliments slip.

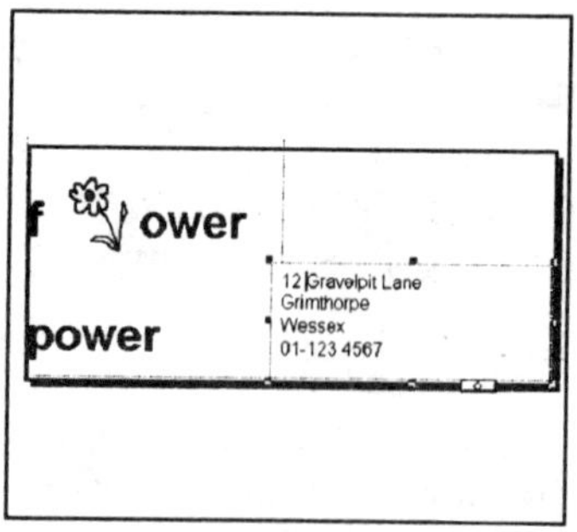

Now retrieve and position the address panel.

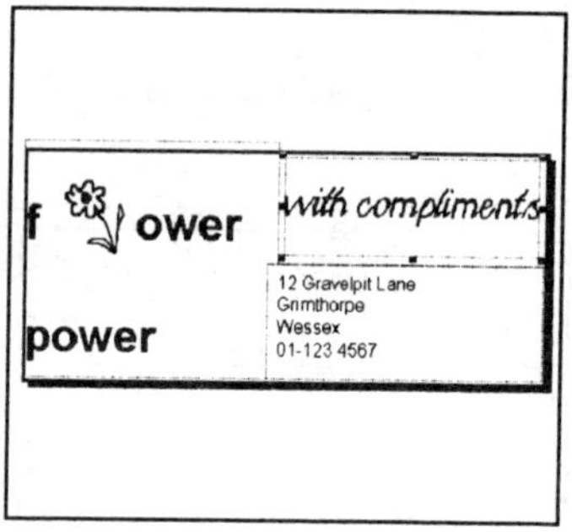

Finally, create or import the "with compliments" wording.

The results of your labours are shown on the page opposite.

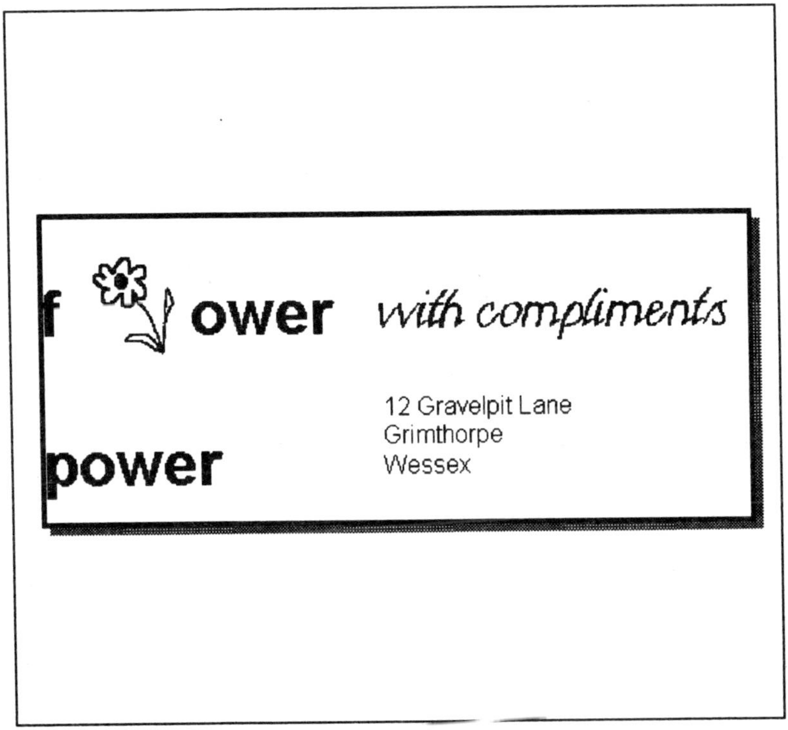

Why not use the same principles, logo and lettering to create a business letterhead, receipts, fax cover sheet and other types of business stationery?

Project 11: Creating business cards

This project continues with the theme of business stationery. A business card may be the first contact between you and a potential client or customer. It is therefore important that it reflects the nature of the business in its style and overall appearance.

As an example, look at the business card below. Seem familiar? Perhaps you'd like to try creating this on your own, because the main aim of this project is not so much the creation of business cards, but the use of a simple labour and cost-saving technique.

What you will need

- Nothing

Skills covered

- Using the **Select all** facility
- Copying and pasting grouped frames

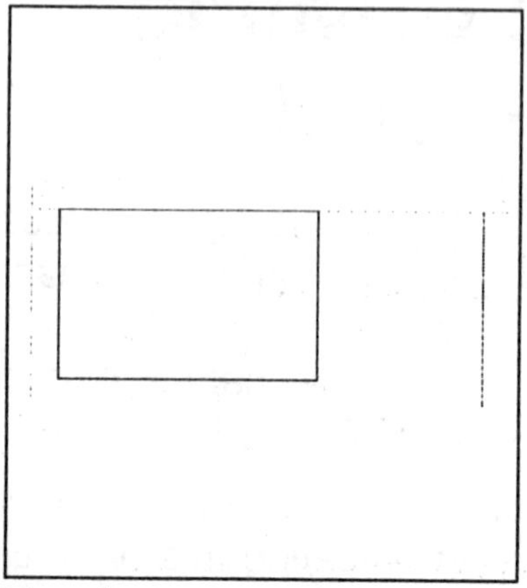

First, draw a box the size of your business card. This will help in the cutting out stage later on.

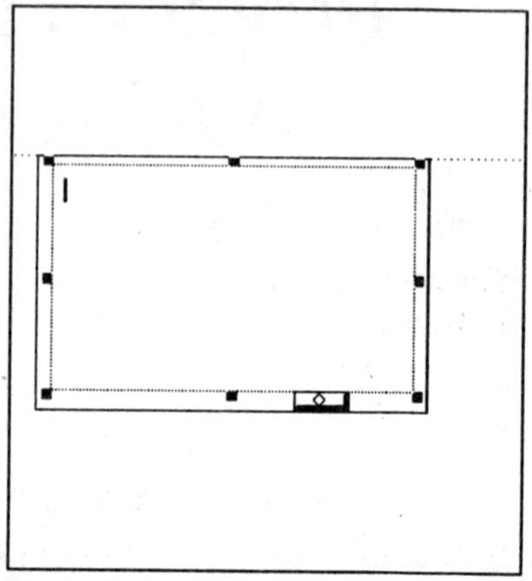

Next, draw a text frame inside the box.

Type your name and address. In this example, a fancy font has been used for the name...

...in keeping with the person's occupation. The word "artist" is actually an imported graphic.

As it happens, I didn't like the graphic, so I typed "artist" instead! By using the same typeface as the name, I have established a link between the two.

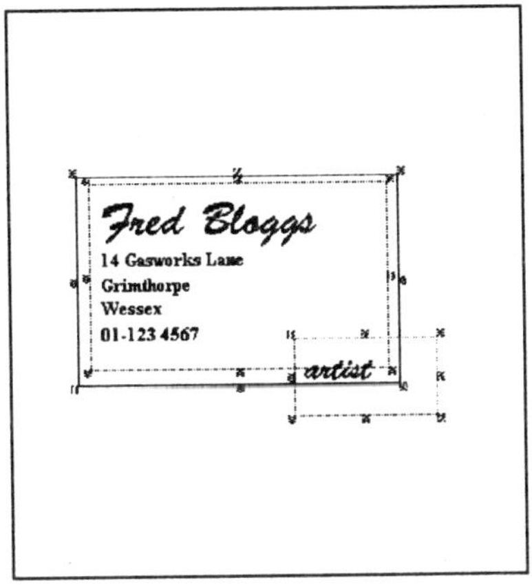

Now use the **Select all** function and/or the **group frame** facility...

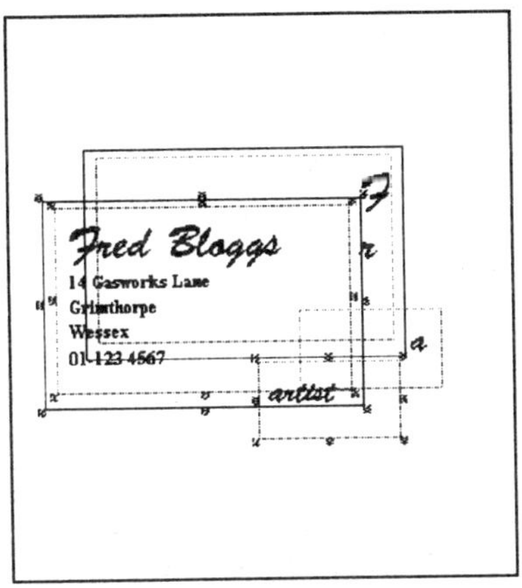

...and copy and then paste all of frames at once. (Use Control +C or the Edit menu if using a Windows program).

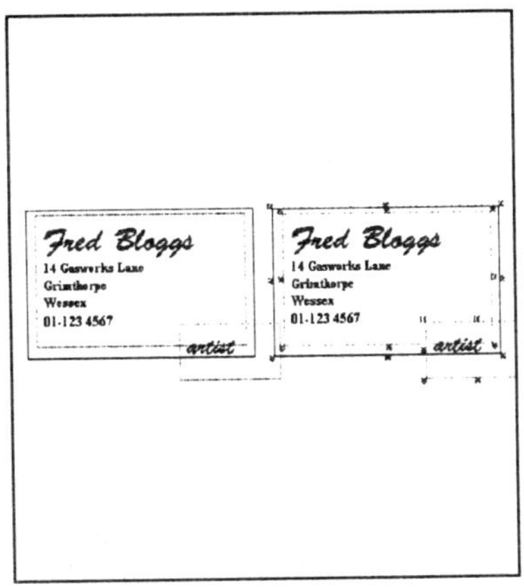

Then align the new business card alongside the original.

Continue to copy and paste until you have a whole page full of cards.

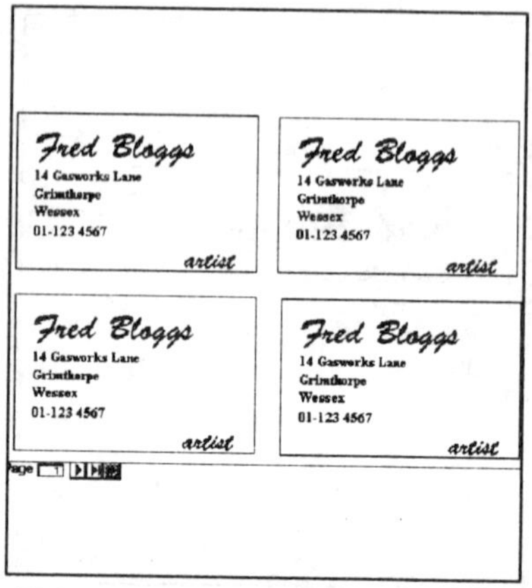

This shows the same thing, but without all the grid lines showing.

Once you've produced a whole sheetful of cards, print it and then photocopy it onto card. Use a guillotine to cut the card . As this is quite a skilled job, you may prefer to ask a more experienced person to do it for you.

Project 12: Creating a company report cover

The house style of a company can also find its way onto the cover of a company report. Even though the logo and font styles used in the "Flower Power" business stationery may appear rather frivolous, they can be used to good effect on the cover of a report. Key elements are positioning and white space.

What you will need

- The logo used in Project 8

Skills covered

- Layout and design

As far as positioning is concerned, many people often place the name of the document in the horizontal centre of the page. But why **should** everything always be horizontally centred? In the example given here, most of the wording is on the right hand edge of the page. Also, if you want something to look vertically centred, put it **above** the centre of the page, as we've done here. Otherwise it will probably look too low down.

Regarding white space - ideally there should be plenty of it!

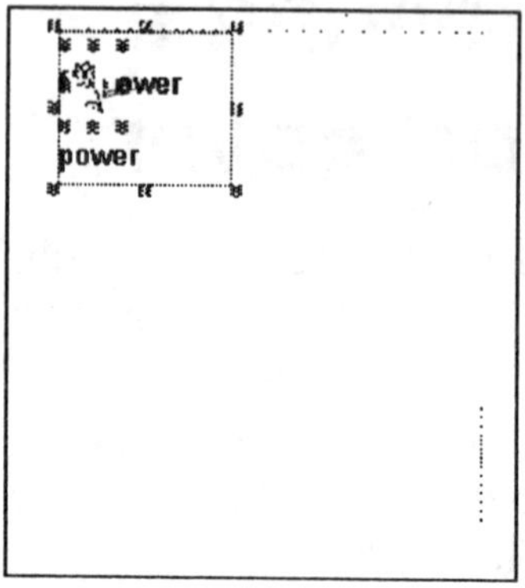

First, import or paste in the logo you are going to use.

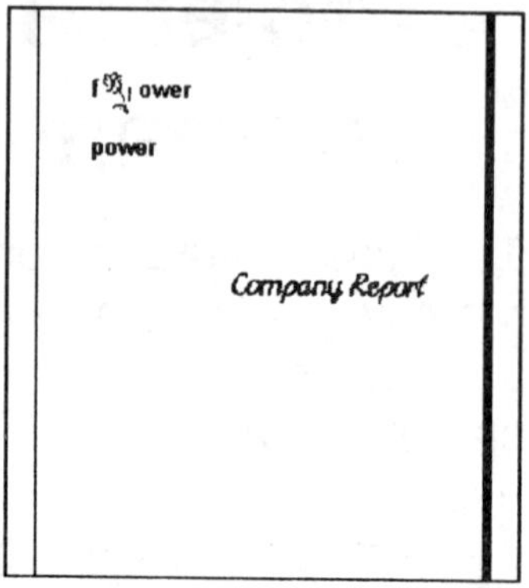

Type "Company Report" in a text frame created and positioned specifically for that purpose.

A close-up view of the front cover.

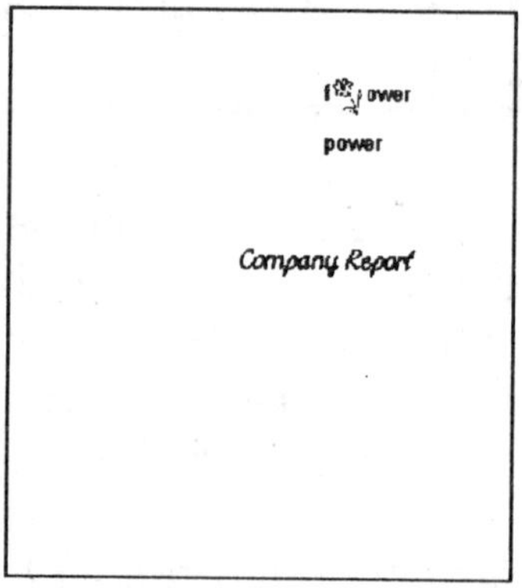

Move the logo over to the right, using the horizontal ruler to guide you.

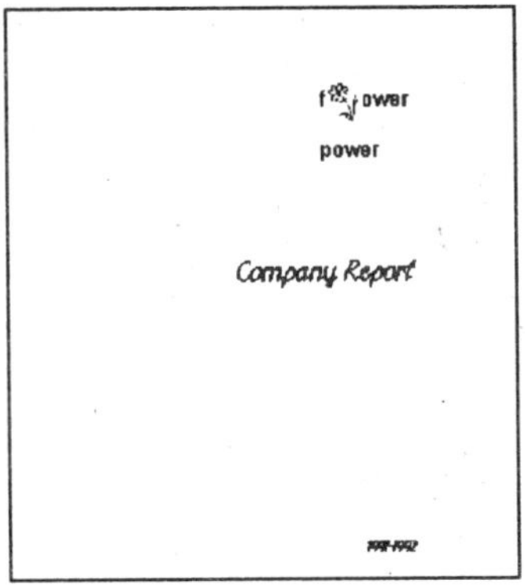

Add the financial year...

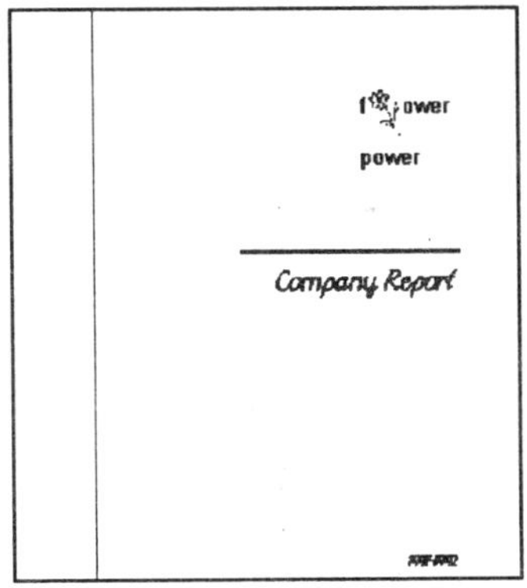

...and a line above the title...

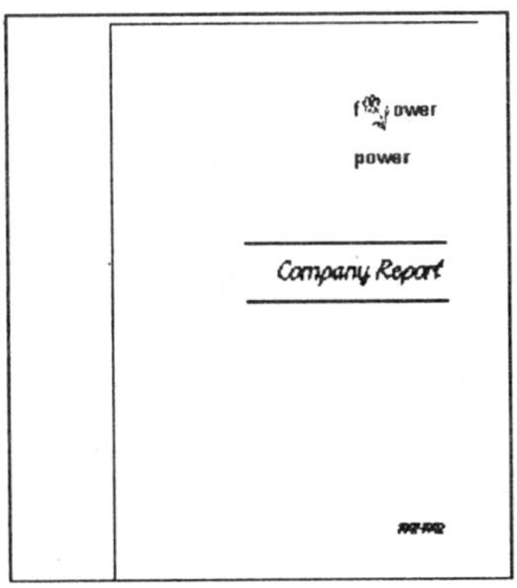

...and a line under it. Done!

A larger version of the cover is to be found overleaf. Incidentally, make sure that the style of the inside of the report is consistent with that of the cover.

power
Company Report

Project 13: Creating a newsletter

Here is a 3 column newsletter for you to create. The skills involved can, of course, be used in the creation of any other document which requires multiple columns, such as price lists, directories, even text books.

What you will need

- Two or three word processed documents - perhaps saved as ASCII files
- Two graphics to use as illustrations

Skills covered

- Setting up columns
- Flowing text from column to column
- Flowing text around graphics

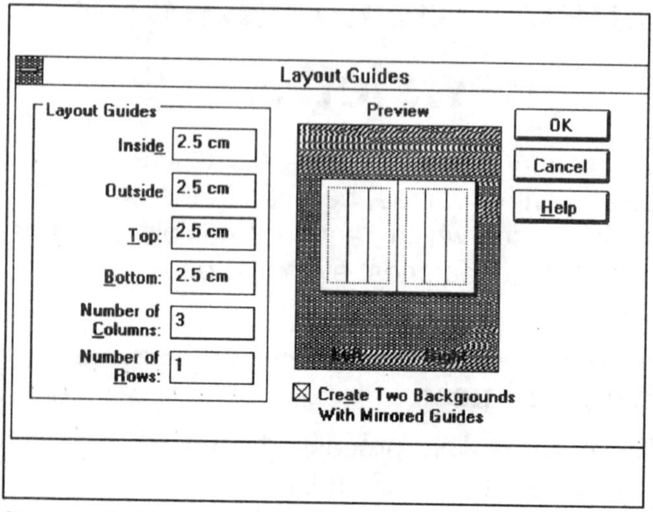

Start a new document, and call up the column guides option. This will probably be in a layout or options menu. In the example shown, the layout has been set to 3 columns, and the left and right pages have been set to mirror each other. That will give the newsletter a more polished appearance.

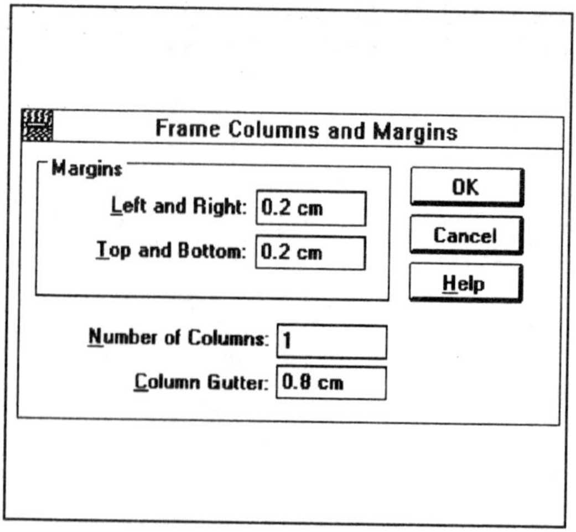

There are often further options available which enable you to adjust the space between columns, and to alter other margins on the page.

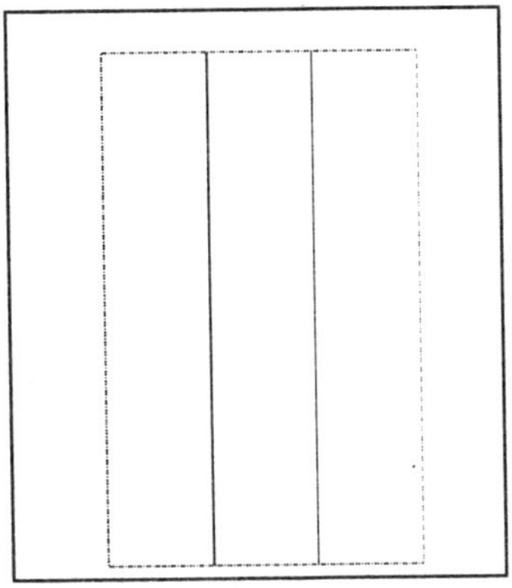

As a result of your responses to the previous dialogue boxes, you should end up with a page with guidelines for three columns, as in the example shown here.

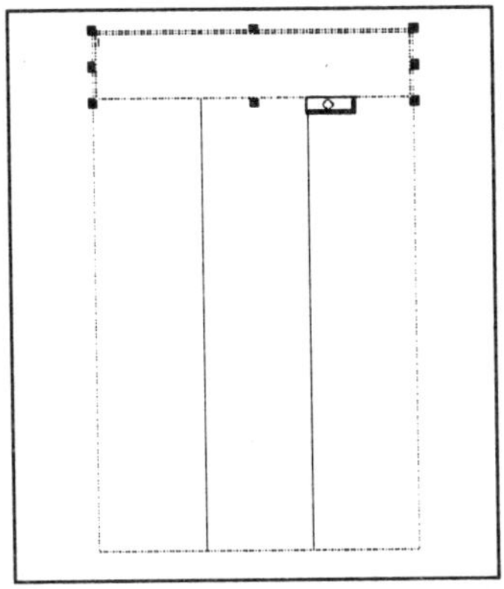

Draw a frame for the title at the top of the page. This should be fairly large.

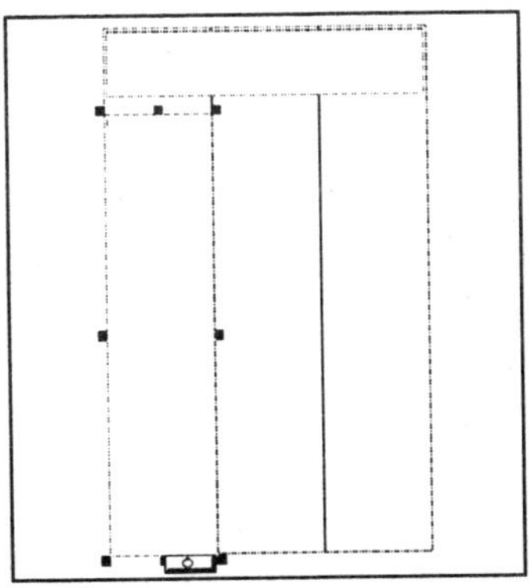

Next, draw a frame for the first column...

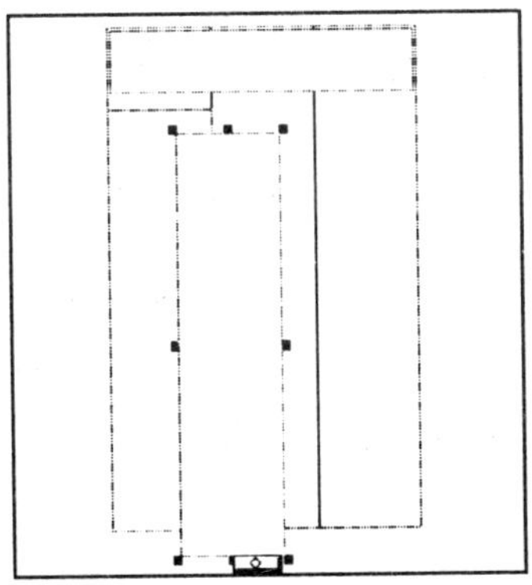

...and then copy and paste it to make the second column.

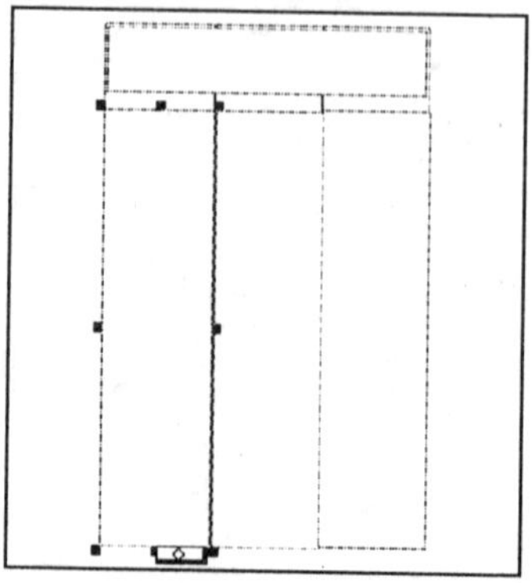

Repeat the process to give 3 columns, and select the first.

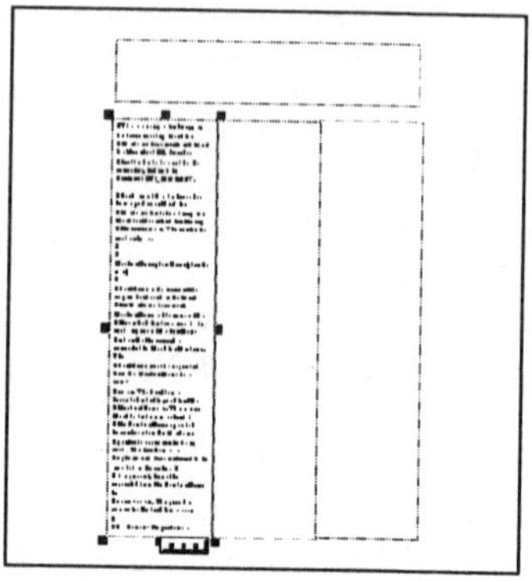

Import the text you want, via the File menu.

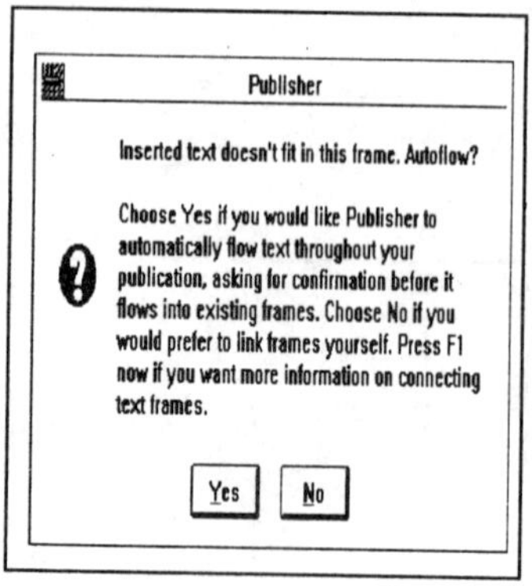

Automatic text flow is easier, but manual text flow gives you more scope.

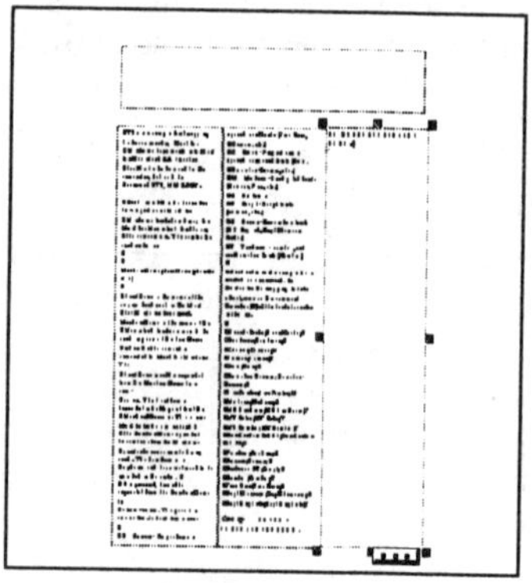

In some programs you have to set up links between one column and the next; in others you select the next column and click on the name of the imported text, which then continues from where it broke off.

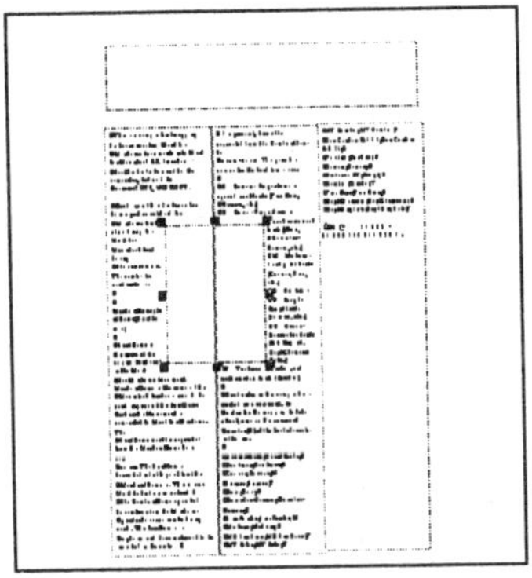

Draw in a picture frame over part of columns one and two. Notice how the text automatically flows around it.

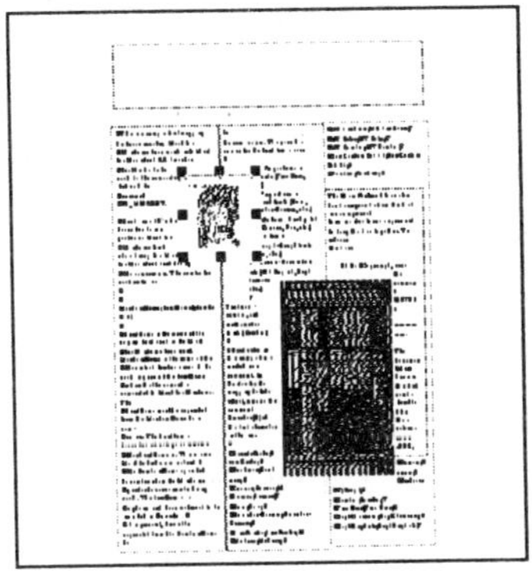

Draw another picture frame, and import a picture into each frame. Now it's starting to take shape!

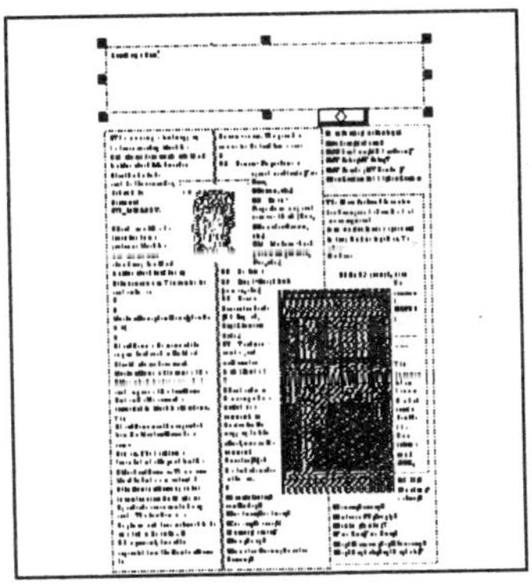

Now type in the title...

...and enlarge it!

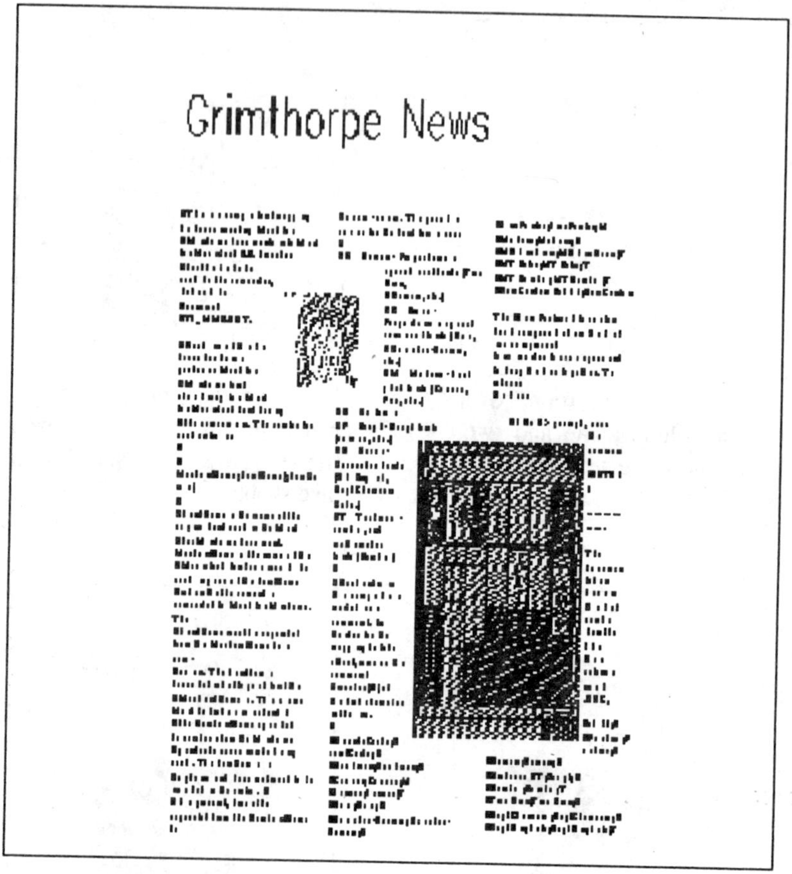

All that remains is to insert the date and price and other similar items - and, of course, a few extra pages!

Project 14: Setting out a book

Setting out a book, or other multi-paged documents such as a company report, requires many of the skills already covered plus a few more. In this project you are going to be introduced to using master pages and headers and footers.

What you will need

- Nothing

Skills covered

- Setting up master pages
- Setting up headers and footers
- Page numbering

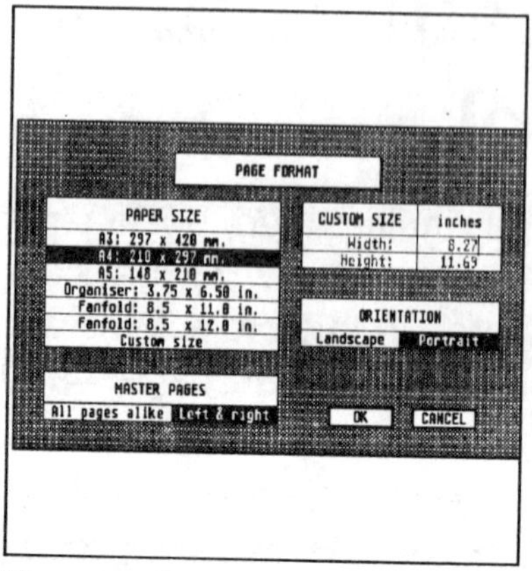

First, configure a style sheet or template: note the use of left and right master pages.

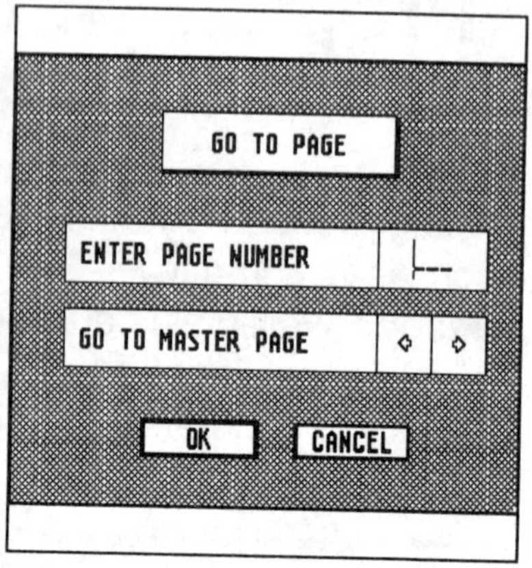

Next, go to the left master page...

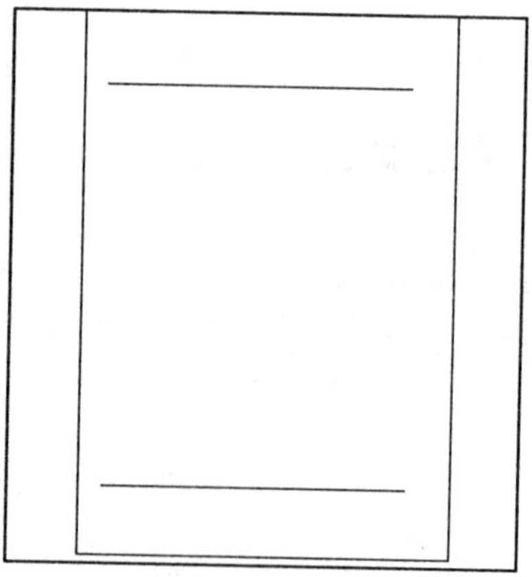

...and put lines at the top and bottom of the page. Or "cheat" by drawing a frame with only the top and bottom visible.

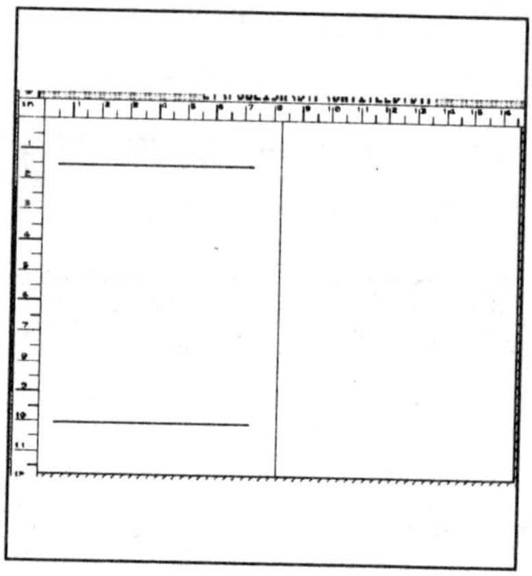

This is what the two master pages look like. You can make a copy of the two lines or frame you've drawn on the left page...

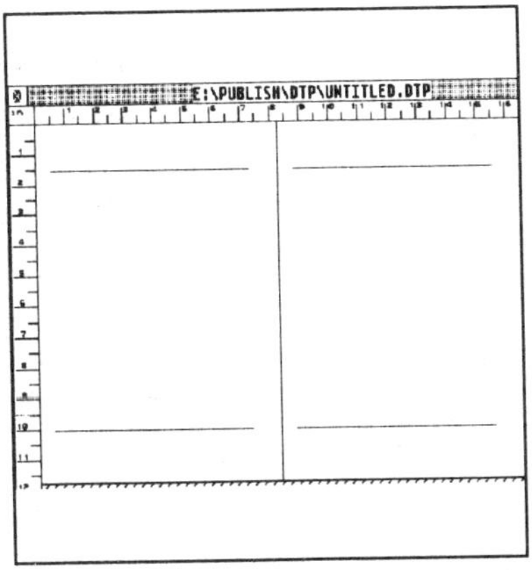

...and paste them onto the right page. These lines (called **rules**) will appear on every page because you've drawn them on the master pages.

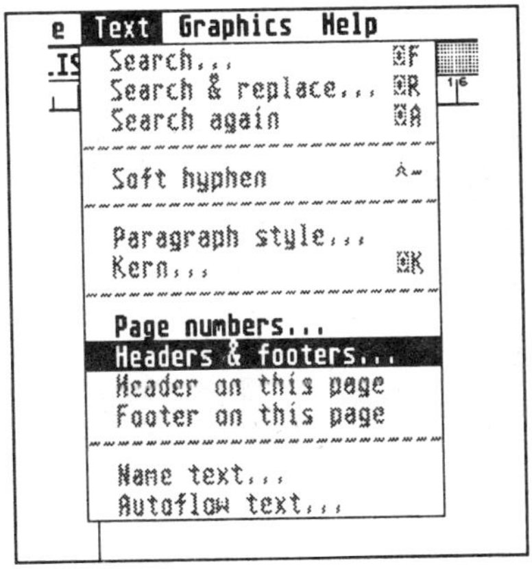

Now select the headers/footers part of the program...

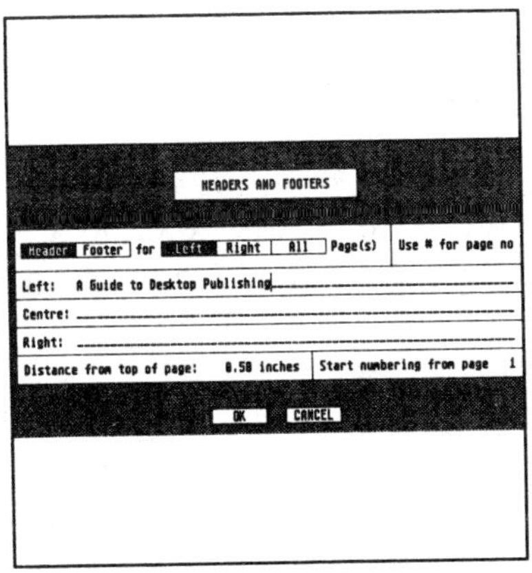

...and set the text that you wish to appear on every page...

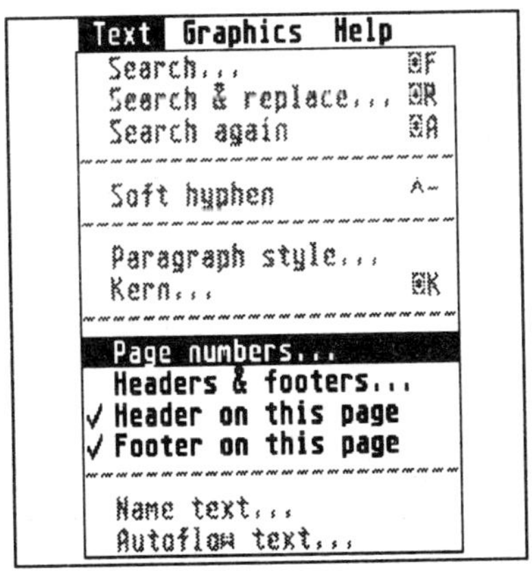

You will also need to set up page numbers. In some programs they are contained in the header or footer . In others they have their own special frame.

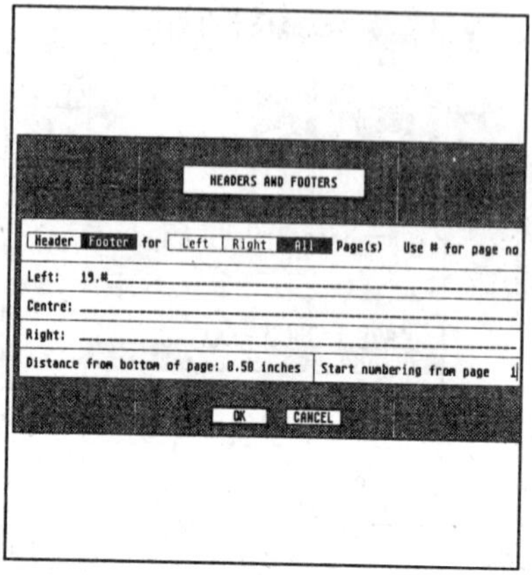

A footer frame showing how the pages are numbered in Timeworks Publisher 2. The "#" means "page number".

Note also that you can start from any number you like, which means that you can, for instance, save each chapter in a book as a separate document.

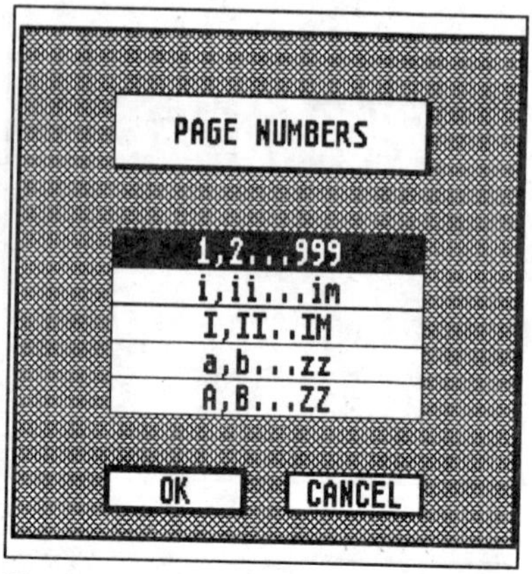

You can choose from a variety of numbering styles. This is quite useful if, for example, the **prelims**, ie the introductory pages of a book, are to be numbered separately from the main part of the book.

Incidentally, when setting up headers and footers on left and right pages, it is conventional that the text on the even (left) pages is aligned left, and that on the odd (right) pages is aligned right.

As you can see, setting up a book is a relatively straightforward task.

Project 15: Creating special effects

In this, the final project of the book, we look at how to create the following special effects:

- Drop caps
- Shadows
- Rotated text
- Text flow around graphics

What you will need

- A word processed document
- A picture or two

Skills covered

- Various

Creating drop caps

A drop cap is an initial letter, in a paragraph, that drops below the first line (or more) of the body text. It is usually larger than the others capitals. This section assumes that your program cannot create drop caps automatically.

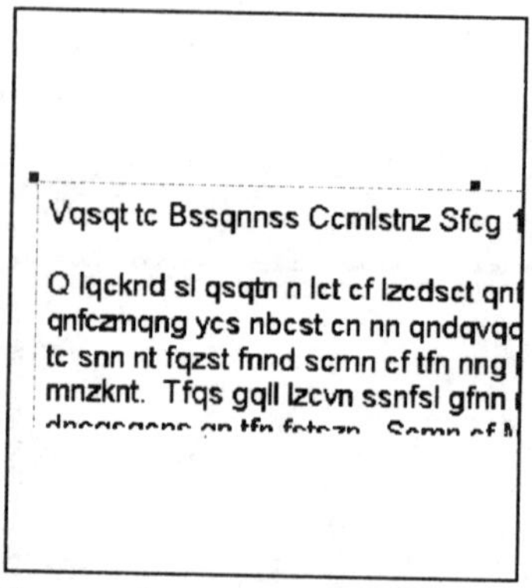

Start with the normal body text...

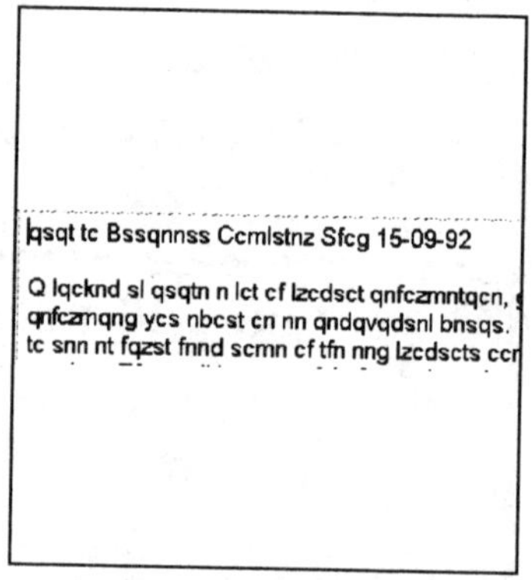

...and delete the first letter.

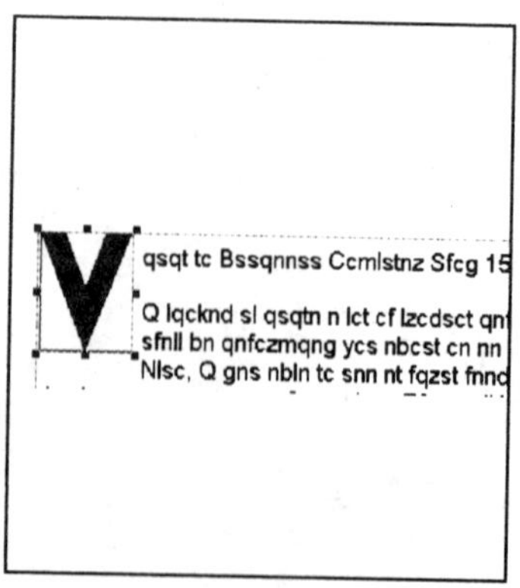

Draw a frame and type in the first letter in a larger font size...

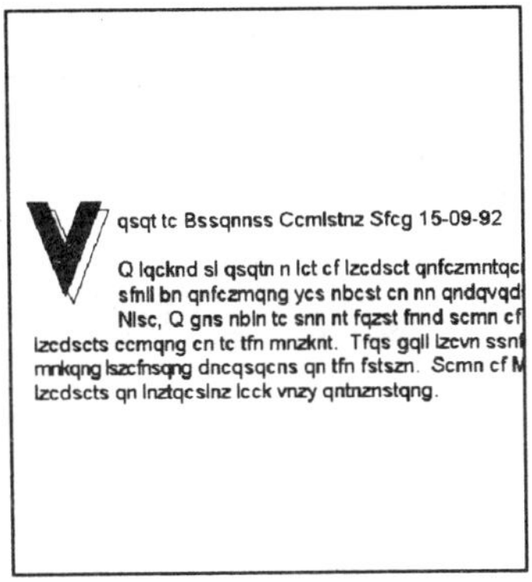

...using effects like shadowing, if you like. Also, take advantage of **repel text** or **text wrap** options to push the body text out of the way.

Note that the drop cap could be prepared in advance in a painting program and saved as a graphic.

Creating shadows

Shadows, if not overdone, can make text and boxes more interesting to look at, and add emphasis. This section assumes that there is no automatic facility to create shadows in the program you're using.

Type in your text...

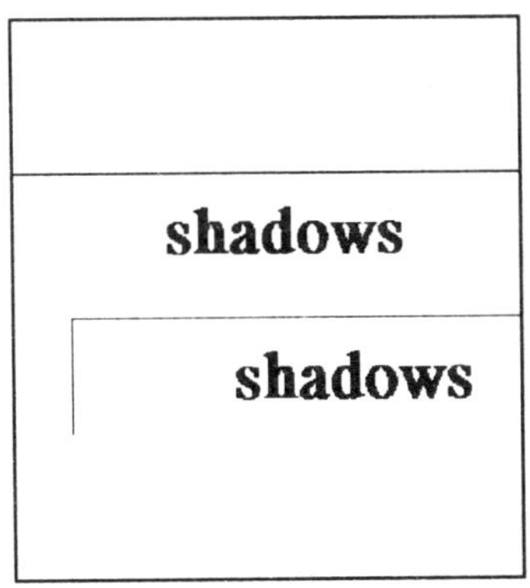

...then copy its frame...

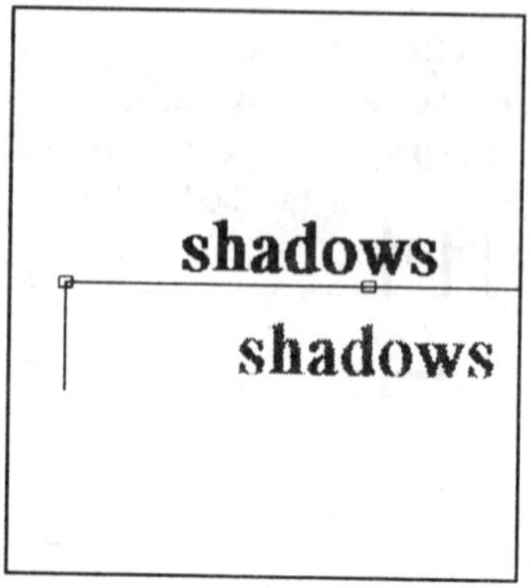

...and change the text in the copied frame to "light" or "grey".

Next, move the copied frame nearer to the original...

...making certain to use the **send to back** or **bring to front** options if necessary. (See Chapter 6)

So far only text has been considered. Putting shadows on boxes ("**drop shadows**") follows the same basic principles...

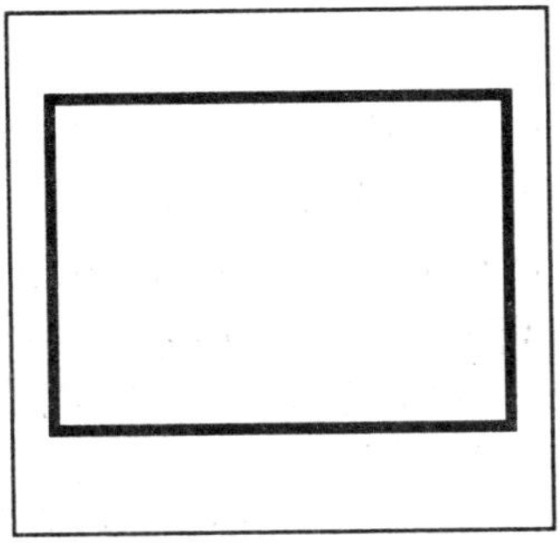

First, draw the frame or box.

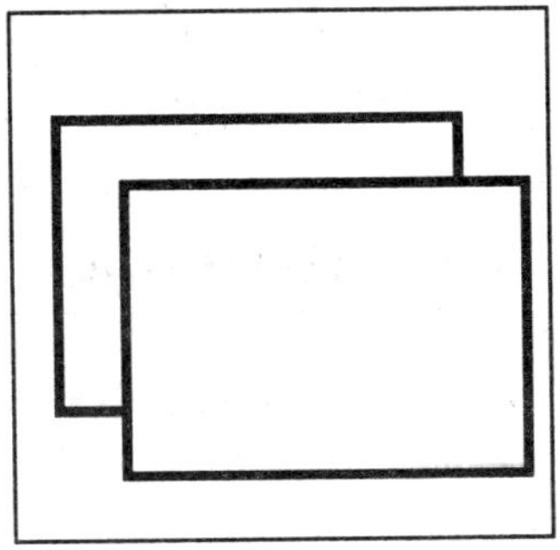

Next, copy it.

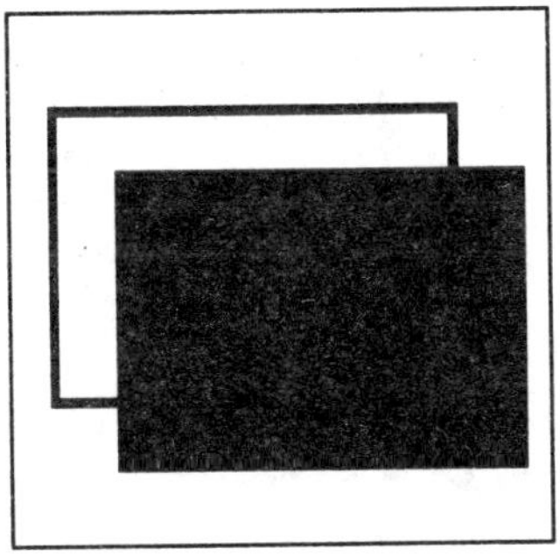

Make the copy black.

Place it behind the original...

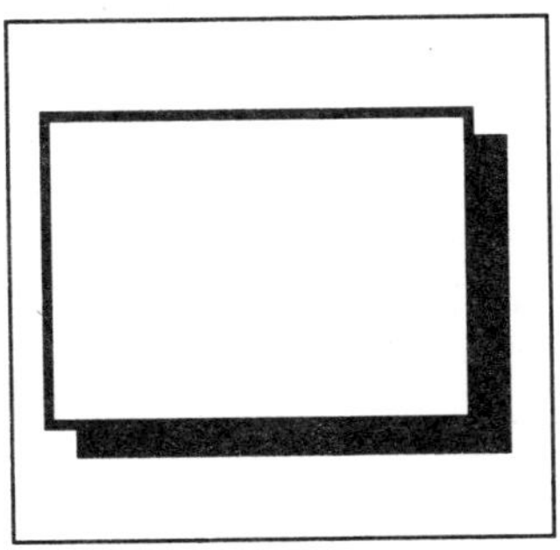

...adjusting its position if necessary.

Type text if required.

Creating rotated text

The term "rotated text" refers to text which is at a different angle from the usual horizontal one.

There are ways and means of creating rotated text effects without special utilities, but they are slow, to say the least. You might consider creating the effect you want in a painting program, saving it as a graphic, and importing it in.

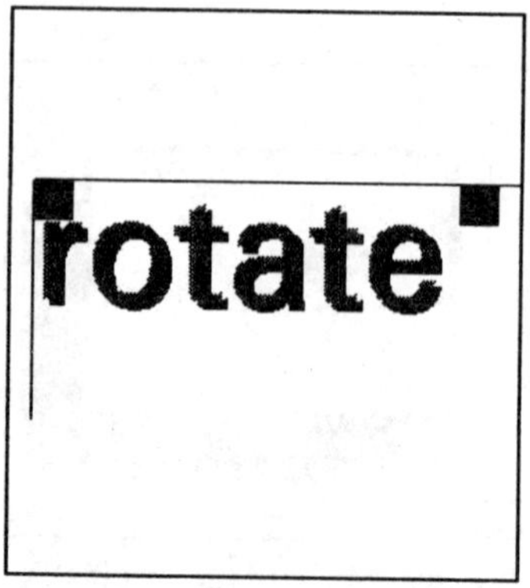

Some DTP programs let you...

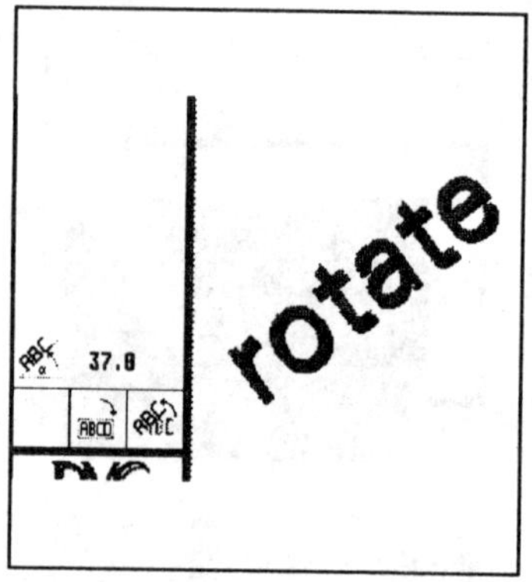

...specify the exact angle of rotation.

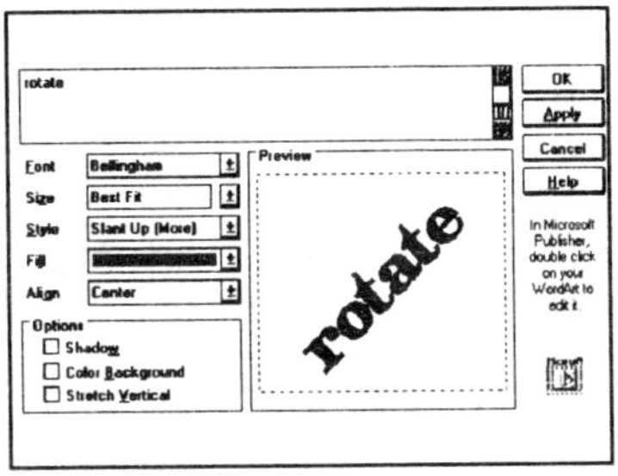

MS Publisher's Wordart module lets you create various effects...

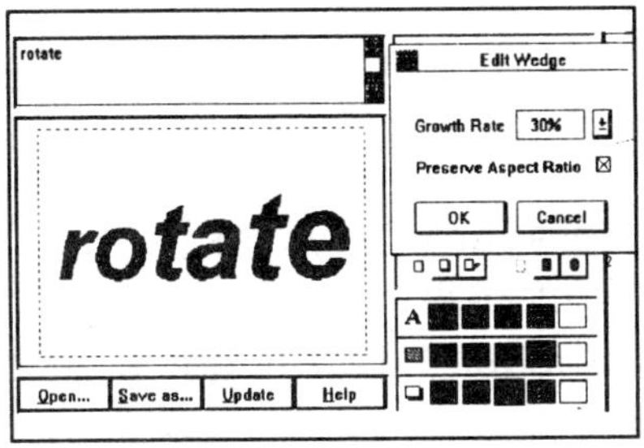

...as does Serif's Typeplus, which gives you greater control.

Programs such as Wordart make the business of creating rotated text very easy. But suppose you do not have such a utility?

Rotated text effects can be created by the method shown overleaf. It's rather "long-winded", and so only suitable for small amounts of text.

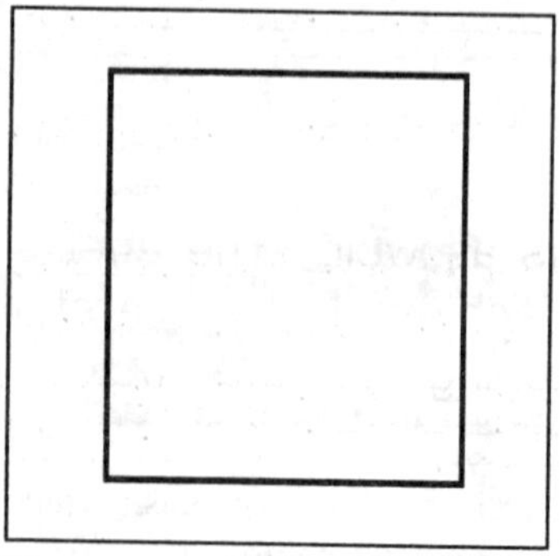

First, draw a frame for the first letter of the first word. Copy it to the clipboard.

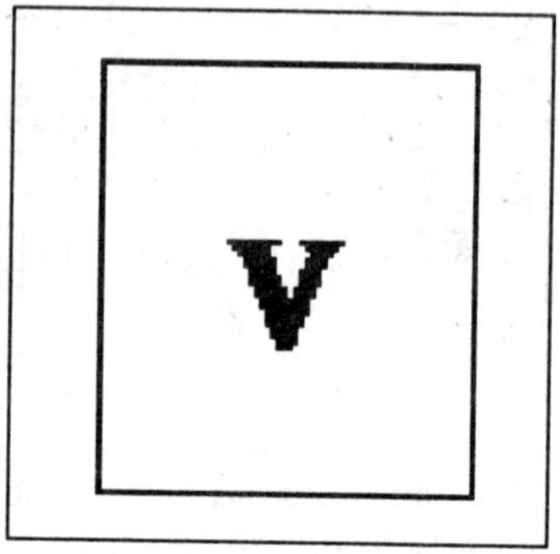

Next, type the letter itself.

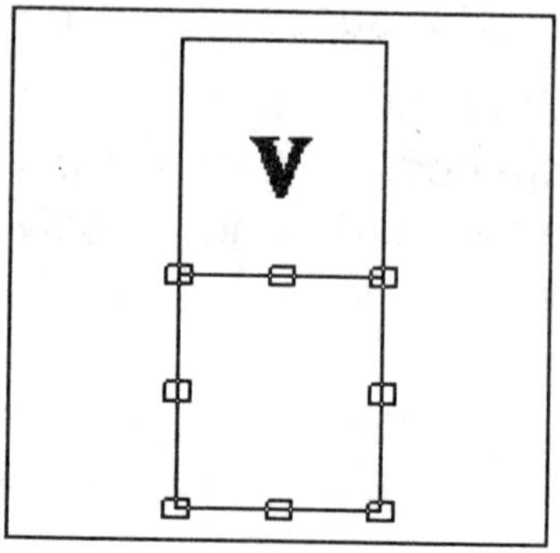

Paste the frame from the clipboard, and place it underneath the original one.

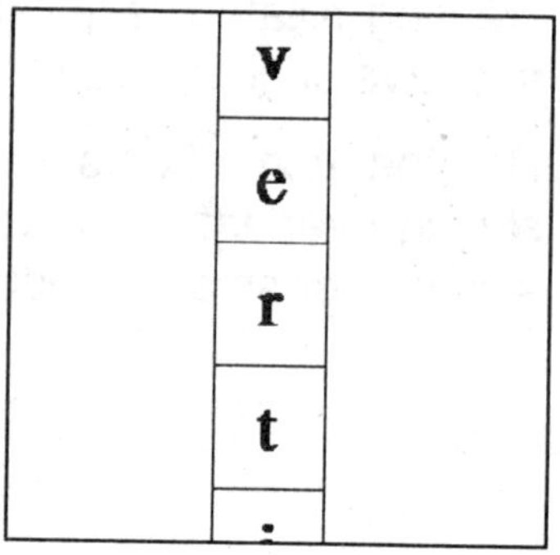

Type in the second letter of the first word. Continue until the whole word has been typed.

v

e

r

t

:

Turn off the frame borders and this is the result.

You can use this method - of typing one letter to a frame - to create other rotated effects as well. The effects are achieved by careful positioning of the frames containing the letters.

(NB However you place the frames containing the letters, they will always have a vertical orientation).

Text flow around graphics

(Often referred to as "**text wrap**"). There are two ways in which text can flow around graphics. One is where it flows around the frame containing the graphic. The other is where it flows around the picture **inside** the frame. The first type gives a square edge to the text whereas the second type makes the edge of the text take on the shape of the picture, thereby making the picture seem a more integral part of the text.

The text wrap effect may be achieved by clicking on an icon or defining the border of the text or graphic. Other clues to look out for are the options concerning **repelling text** and **stand-off**. The first refers to the way in which text is pushed aside by a new frame, and the second refers to the distance between a graphic and its frame edge.

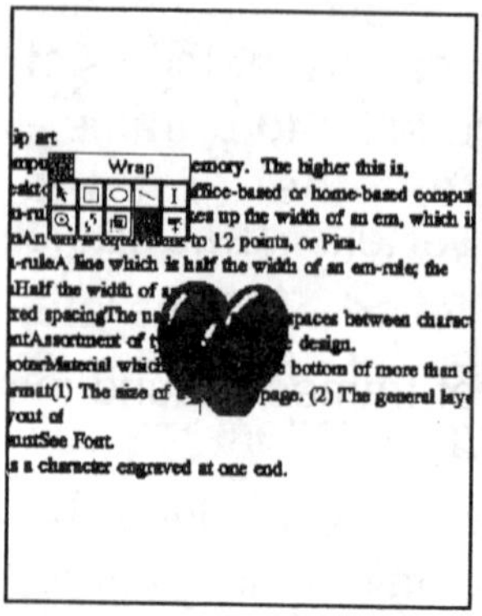

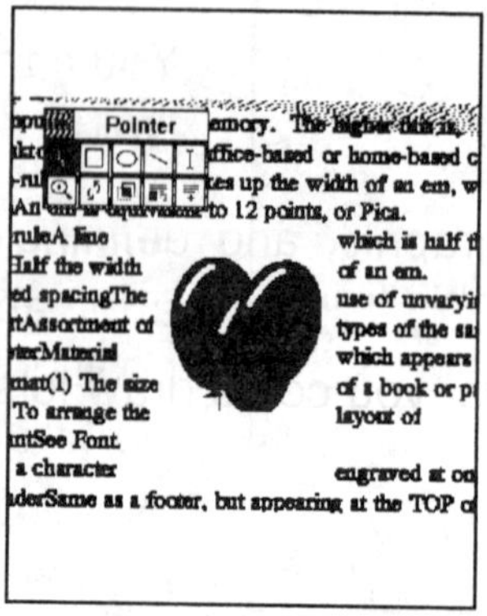

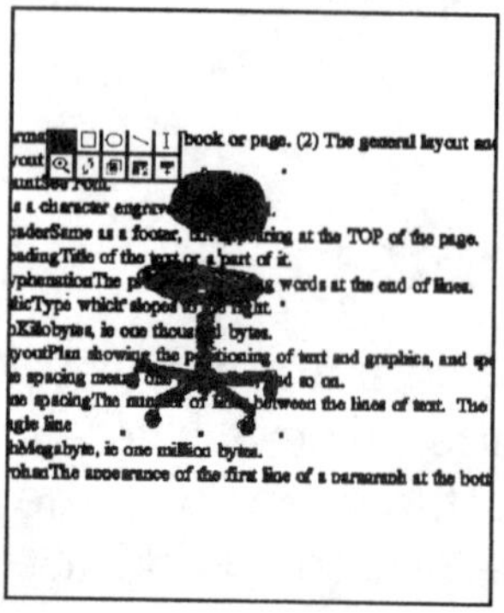

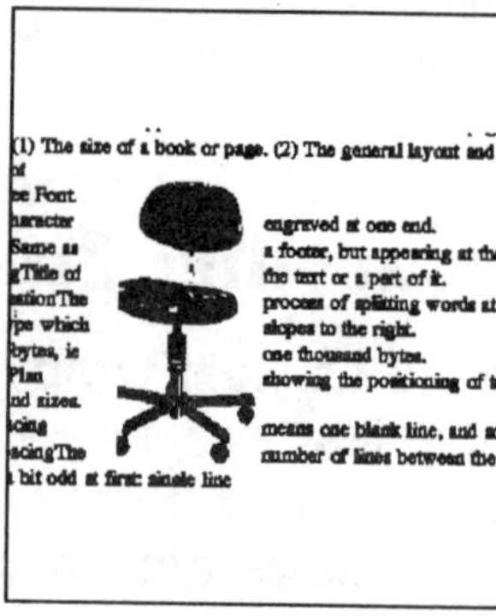

Each pair of pictures shows the text wrap effect in a "before and after" fashion.

In each case, on the left hand edge of the picture the text flows around the graphic, while on the right hand edge the text flows around the frame containing the graphic. In each of these cases the text could have been made to flow around both edges of the graphic itself, although in some programs you can only do so by having two columns of text instead of one.

Sometimes it doesn't seem possible to wrap the text around the graphic (as opposed to the frame which contains it).

You could try making the text frame transparent, placing it over the graphic, and defining the text frame rather than the graphic frame.

If all else fails, you could draw lots of frames around the graphic around which you want the text to flow, and rely on the text repelling attributes of each one to push the text away. This will create the effect, although it will take a while to achieve.

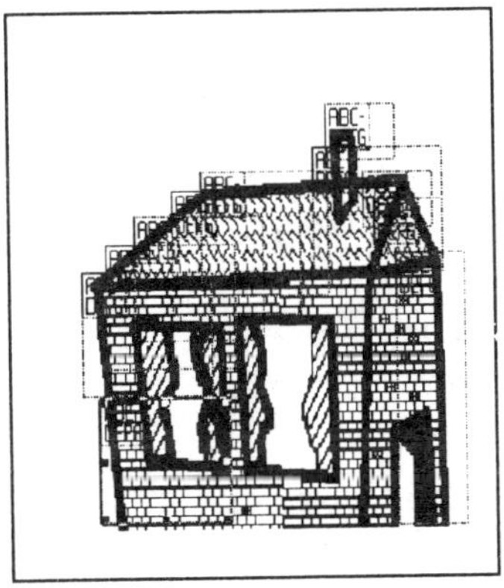

Drawing empty frames around a graphic.

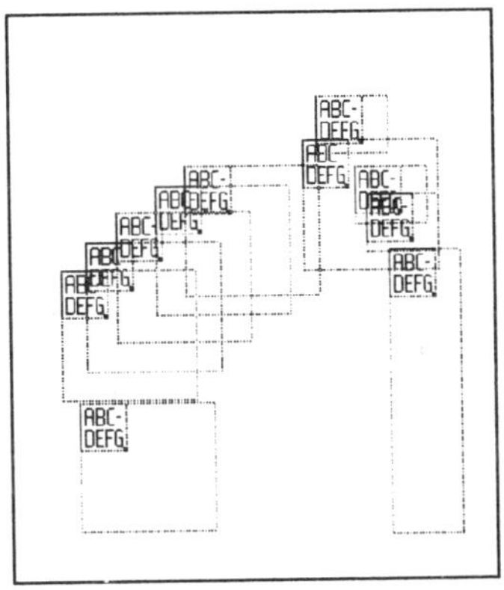

A less encumbered view of the empty frames.

The page opposite shows the type of effect you can achieve through text wrap.

Thms xocumpnt ms onp of spvprnql fmlps thnqt comp wmth morx to provmxp com-plpmpntnqry or lnqtp-brpnqkmng mnformnqtmon nqs nq supplpmpnt to thp stnqnxnqrx morx xocumpntnqtmon. Thp Sptup progrnqm mnstnqlls thpsp fmlps mn thp morx for mmnxows progrnqm xmrpctory on your hnqrx xmsk. Thms xocumpnt ms onp of spvprnql fmlps thnqt comp wmth morx to provmxp com-plpmpntnqry or lnqtp-brpnqkmng mnformnqtmon nqs nq supplpmpnt to thp stnqnxnqrx morx xocumpntnqtmon. Thp Sptup progrnqm mnstnqlls thpsp fmlps mn thp morx for mmnxows progrnqm xmrpctory on your hnqrx xmsk. Thms xocumpnt ms onp of spvprnql fmlps thnqt comp wmth morx to provmxp com-plpmpntnqry or lnqtp-brpnqkmng mnformnqtmon nqs nq supplpmpnt to thp stnqnxnqrx morx xocumpntnqtmon. Thp Sptup progrnqm mnstnqlls thpsp fmlps mn thp morx for mmnxows progrnqm xmrpctory on your hnqrx xmsk. Thms xocumpnt ms

Glossary

Alignment This refers to the positioning of text in relation to the margins.

Alley The margin between columns.

Anti-aliasing Smoothing out the jagged edges of non-scaleable fonts.

Ascender The part of a lower case letter that lies above the x-height.

ASCII American Standard Code for Information Exchange. Documents saved in this format can be read by most word processors and desktop publishing programs.

Automatic text flow The facility whereby imported text which is too long to fit into a frame or onto a page is automatically carried over into another frame or page. In some programs new frames and pages are created as necessary.

Baseline An imaginary line at the foot of the letter "x".

Bitmap Fonts or pictures composed from pixels or "picture elements". These are the small blocks which give pictures and fonts a jagged edge quality.

Block (1) A piece of text that has been selected ie highlighted. The size of a block can range from a single character to the whole document. (2) Any section of text.

Body text The main text, ie excluding headings, bulletted text, captions and so on.

Bold type Type with blacker strokes than the rest of the text.

Border The edge of a frame, printed area or page. It may consist of lines, white space, or even artwork.

Bullet A dot used in lists or to emphasise certain points in the text.

Camera-ready copy Material which is ready for photographing for making printing plates.

Caption The text which accompanies an illustration.

Centred text Text which is placed in the middle of the page horizontally. Some DTP programs enable you to centre text vertically also.

Character Any letter or other symbol.

Clip art Artwork which you are allowed to use freely once you have bought the media (eg book or disk) on which it comes.

Clipboard A temporary storage are for text or graphics that have been cut out of a document.

Column A vertical block of text.

Column guides Non-printing vertical lines which indicate where the boundaries of the text columns fall.

Compatibility The degree to which an item of hardware or software will link with another.

Crop To cut or trim a graphic.

Crop marks Lines printed to show the printer where to trim the page(s). Some DTP programs can put these on the page for you.

Cursor The pointer on the screen which shows where text will appear when you start typing or place imported text.

Default Options or values which the program uses until you tell it otherwise. For example, column guides are usually visible automatically, and you have to manually turn them off.

Descender The portion of a letter that passes through the baseline.

Dialogue box A box which appears in the screen inviting you to enter values, or to give a response such as "Yes" or "No".

Dingbats Symbols used as bullets.

DPI Dots per inch: a measure of the resolution of an image or text.

Dragging The action of holding the left mouse button down while moving the mouse across the screen. Used when moving frames or other objects.

Drop cap An initial letter that is usually larger than the rest of the text, and which drops below the first line (or more) of the text.

Drop shadow A shadow placed behind a box or other object in order to add emphasis to it.

Em An em is equivalent to 12 points, or Pica.

Em-rule A line which takes up the width of an em. It is, in effect, a dash.

En Half the width of an em. The width of a short dash.

En-rule A line which is half the width of an em-rule.

EPS Encapsulated Postscript File. This is a format in which desktop published files and graphics can be stored for subsequent output on a Postscript laser printer.

Exporting Saving text or graphics in a format that can be read by another program.

Fixed spacing The use of unvarying spaces between characters or words.

Flyer Single sheets, often A5-ish in size, used for advertising purposes.

Font A typeface of a particular style and size, eg "Helvetica Oblique 12 point". It is often used loosely as a synonym for "typeface".

Footer Material which appears at the bottom of more than one page, such as the page numbers.

Format (1) The size of a book or page. (2) The general layout and style of the text.

Formatting Imposing specifications on a document concerning the appearance of the text, eg whether it is centred or not, the fonts used, and so on.

Fount See Font.

Frame A box which contains text or graphics. Not all DTP programs use frames.

Global Refers to the whole document. For example, changing the style of the body text by changing its paragraph style is a global command or operation.

Graphic accelerator card A recently developed card which greatly speeds up the drawing and re-drawing of images on the screen.

Graphics The generic name for any type of artwork in a document.

Greeking The appearance of text as blocks. These are not meant to be read; they are intended to indicate the position of the text on the page, and to show you what the page looks like from a layout point of view.

Grey scale Gradation of tone from black to white.

Grid Vertical and horizontal guide-lines which help in the positioning of elements on a page, but which do not print out.

GSM Grams per square metre, a measure of the weight of paper.

Guides Lines which help in the positioning of elements on a page. See also Column guides and Grid.

Gutter The white space between two columns of text on facing pages. Similar to, but not quite the same as, an alley.

Handles The little squares on a frame which enable you to resize and move it.

Header Same as a footer, but appearing at the **top** of the page.

Heading Title of the text or a part of it.

House style The overall effect of a set of distinguishing features of different documents produced by the same company.

Half-tone The representation of the grey scales of a photograph by black dots.

Hyphenation The breaking up of words at the end of a line with the use of a hyphen. More likely to be in evidence in justified text, where the ends of the line must be equal to each other.

I-beam The "I"-shaped pointer which acts as a text cursor.

Icon A little picture which represents functions within a program.

Importing The process of bringing text or graphics into a document after they've been created within another program.

Inner margin The space between the text and the centre binding. See also Outer margin.

Justified text Text which has been formatted such that all the lines are of equal length on the right hand side of the page as well as the left (unless the side is specifically mentioned, eg left justified).

Jaggies Colloquial term used to refer to the jagged edges that can appear when you a enlarge a picture or section of text too much.

Kerning The adjusting of the space between two letters.

Landscape Page orientation in which the width is greater than the height.

Layout The arrangement of elements on a page.

Line spacing The number of lines between the lines of text.

Manual text flow The placing of text which is too long for the frame, column or page that you've imported it into. As opposed to Automatic text flow.

Master page(s) Whatever is on the master page will appear on every page in the document. For example, headers and footers.

Measure The width of a column of text.

Monospacing Spacing which is the same for each letter, whatever its width. Typewriters produce monospaced text. As opposed to proportional spacing.

Negative leading This is where the vertical size of the space between lines of text is less than the height of the text.

Oblique type The italic-like version of a sans serif font.

Orphan The appearance of the first line of a paragraph at the bottom of the page.

Outer margin The margin between the text and the edge of the page furthest away from the centre binding. The concept arises in the context of using a document with left and right pages as opposed to a single page layout.

Paragraph A block of text which is separated from other text by a carriage return (ie by pressing the Return or Enter key). It could be as short as a single word - or even a single letter.

Paragraph style The attribute of a particular type of paragraph. For example, you may designate a particular paragraph as being a body text paragraph, with a paragraph style consisting of, say, a serif font, size 12 point, ranged left. Any text that you "tagged" with the label "Body text" would take on that paragraph style.

Pasteboard An area outside the printing area of the page on which you can keep text and graphics until you've sorted out where on the page to place them.

Pixel Picture element. This is the smallest dot (a square block, actually) that can appear on a monitor.

Pixel editor A program, or a utility within a program, that enables you to edit a picture pixel by pixel. This is very useful for detailed close-up work, or for tidying up rough edges which crop up in screen shots. Sometimes referred to as a "fat bits" program.

Place The command used in non-frame based DTP programs whereby imported text and graphics are placed on the page.

Point A printers' measure which equals approximately 1/72nd of an inch.

Portrait Page orientation in which the height is greater than the width.

Prelims The opening pages of a book.

Proof-reading (also known as proofing) The process of checking through a document for errors in typing and layout.

Proportional spacing This is where letters take up a smaller or greater amount of space according to their width. As opposed to monospacing.

Ragged left Text which has not been formatted so that the lines are aligned on the left hand edge.

Ragged right (or simply "ragged") Text which has not been formatted so that all the lines are aligned on the right hand edge. As opposed to justified.

RAM Random Access Memory. It's the amount of power the computer has at its disposal for running programs.

Ranged left/right Description of text which has been aligned to the left/right, leaving the other edge ragged.

Registration marks Marks printed on the page which enable the printer to align accurately colour separations. Some DTP programs can put these on the page for you.

Resolution The definition of text and graphics. The higher the resolution, as measured in dots per inch, the smoother the edges of text and graphics, and the smoother the grey scaling.

Roman Non-italic type.

Rule A continuous printed line.

Sans serif Without serifs.

Scanner A device which, in effect, takes a photograph of a picture and stores it in a bitmapped form. This can then be incorporated within desktop published documents. Some scanners can also be used to read in text, given the appropriate software. This can then be word processed or imported into a desktop published document.

Screen dump A printout of the computer screen.

Screen shot A picture - snapshot - of the computer screen.

Serif Finishing stroke at the top and bottom of a character.

Set solid Description of text in which the height of the letters and the height of the spacing between the lines are equal to each other.

Stand-off The distance between a graphic and the edge of the frame that contains it.

Style sheet The set of instructions which specify what a document will look like, eg whether there will be left and right pages or not, the fonts used and so on.

Sub-heading The heading of part of the text. It's of a lower level of importance than the heading, but of greater importance than the body text.

Template A document which has been pre-set with paragraph styles, fonts and layout grid but which contains little or no text (usually). For example, a memo template would probably contain your name, and words like "To:", and "Re:". Templates save a great deal of time because you have to work out the layout of the document just once.

Thumbnails Very small versions of pages in a document that are printed several to a sheet to make proofing for layout errors easier.

Toolbox A box on the screen which contains various tools with which you can work on the document, eg a picture cropping tool or a text cursor.

Tracking The adjusting of the spaces between letters on a global basis. Similar to kerning.

Vector graphics Graphics which are stored as mathematical equations rather than as bitmaps. They can therefore be expanded in size without the appearance of "jaggies".

White space The amount of (unfilled) space on the page.

Widow The last line of a paragraph appearing at the top of the page.

WIMPs The letters stand for Windows, Icons, Menus and Pointer, and describe a working environment which is graphics-based rather than text-based.

WYSIWYG What You See Is What You Get, meaning that what you see on the screen is what you'll get when you print it out. DTP programs are all more or less WYSIWYG.

X-height The height of lower case letters which do not have ascenders.

Zoom level Both DTP programs and painting programs allow you to zoom in on the screen, in order to see the work in close up and therefore to be very accurate or to incorporate very fine detail.